HOME OFFICE RESEARCH STUDY No.139

Policing domestic violence in the 1990s

by Sharon Grace

A HOME OFFICE
RESEARCH AND PLANNING UNIT
REPORT

LONDON: HMSO

WP 0865221 X

ISBN 0 11 341140 5

HOME OFFICE RESEARCH STUDIES

'Home Office Research Studies' comprise reports on research undertaken in the Home Office to assist in the exercise of its administrative functions, and for the information of the judicature, the services for which the Home Secretary has responsibility (direct or indirect) and the general public.

On the last pages of this report are listed titles already published in this series, in the preceding series *Studies in the Causes of Delinquency and the Treatment of Offenders,* and in the series of *Research and Planning Unit Papers.*

HMSO

Standing order service

Placing an order with HMSO BOOKS enables a customer to receive other titles in this series automatically as published.

This saves time, trouble and expense of placing individual orders and avoids the problem of knowing when to do so.

For details please write to HMSO BOOKS (PC11B.2), Publications Centre, P.O. Box 276, London SW8 5DT and quoting reference 25.08.011.

The standing order service also enables customers to receive automatically as published all material of their choice which additionally saves extensive catalogue research. The scope and selectivity of the service has been extended by new techniques, and there are more than 3,500 classifications to choose from. A special leaflet describing the service in more detail may be obtained on request.

Foreword

Home Office Circular 60/1990 recommended that the police adopt a more interventionist approach to policing domestic violence by arresting assailants where an offence has been committed; by recording and investigating domestic violence cases in the same way as other violent assaults; and by offering protection and support to victims. Forces were also encouraged to set up dedicated units to deal with domestic violence cases, and to liaise with the relevant statutory and voluntary agencies to facilitate a co-ordinated response.

The research reported here examined how far such recommendations are reflected in current police policy and practice and highlighted examples of good practice. An initial telephone survey looked at all forces in England and Wales, following which five forces were examined in detail.

The findings show that while officers have increased their understanding and awareness of domestic violence issues, the transition of policy into practice has been as yet limited. The introduction of Domestic Violence Officers has had a very positive impact on victim satisfaction, but further consideration needs to be given as to how that success can affect the policing of domestic violence by non-specialist officers.

ROGER TARLING
Head of the Research and Planning Unit

Acknowledgements

I am grateful to the Chief Constables who agreed to take part in this study and in particular, those in the five areas chosen for the detailed evaluation - Northamptonshire, Nottinghamshire, South Yorkshire, Thames Valley and West Midlands. Particular thanks are due to my "liaison" officers in each of these forces who were unfailingly helpful and co-operative - DCI Keith Bell, Inspector Dara Lloyd, DCI Roger Macklin, Sergeant Anita McKenzie and Superintendent Gill Read.

I am grateful to the representatives from the other voluntary and statutory agencies who agreed to be interviewed for the study. A great deal of thanks is also due to the victims who agreed to participate.

Thanks are due to Vittoria D'Amore, Anne Dunlop and Rob Hider who helped with the field work. Particular thanks are due to Mary Barker upon whose astute field notes Chapter Seven is largely based.

Finally, I would like to thank my colleagues at the RPU - Carol Hedderman for not only her extremely helpful comments and advice on the final report, but also her tremendous support throughout the whole of the project and Mike Hough for his insight.

SHARON GRACE

Contents

Summary

Home Office circular 60/1990 recommended:

- that the police take a more interventionist approach in domestic violence cases - with a presumption in favour of arrest;

- that domestic violence crimes are recorded and investigated in the same way as other violent crimes; and

- that the police adopt a more sympathetic and understanding attitude towards victims of domestic violence.

Forces were also encouraged to set up dedicated units or appoint officers to deal specifically with domestic violence cases and to liaise with other agencies working in the field.

The research reported here set out to discover how far such recommendations are now reflected in current police policies and practices. An initial telephone survey obtained an overview of policy and practice for 42 of the 43 forces in England and Wales. Five forces were then selected to be studied in detail - Northamptonshire, Nottinghamshire, South Yorkshire, Thames Valley and West Midlands.

Key Findings

The national picture

- At the time of the telephone survey all but three forces had produced a force policy document on domestic violence.

- Just over half of the forces had a specialist unit with <u>some</u> responsibility for domestic violence but only <u>five</u> forces had domestic violence units dedicated solely to this offence.

- Thirty-three forces felt that they had an adequate system for recording and monitoring incidents of domestic violence.

- All but two forces said that they co-operated with other agencies on domestic violence matters.

The police response overall

- Most officers felt that the policing of domestic violence had improved and that such incidents were now being taken more seriously with more positive intervention and more support and advice available for victims. There was evidence that officers had increased their awareness of domestic violence issues and showed a greater understanding and sympathy for victims.

- A third of operational officers (Constables and Sergeants) had not heard of Circular 60/1990 at all and over half said that they had not received any new guidelines on domestic violence - despite their managers' confidence that the guidance had been successfully disseminated. Very few officers had received any training on the policing of domestic violence.

- Although most officers were aware that arrest should be a priority in domestic violence cases, almost half of them put it below all other considerations (e.g. the safety of the victim and any children) when asked to prioritise their actions at a domestic violence scene. Their decision to arrest appeared to be heavily influenced by whether a complainant would support any police action.

- There was little evidence of any systematic recording or monitoring of domestic violence cases. Only a quarter of operational officers said that they were consistently able to check police records for any previous history of assaults before attending a domestic violence incident.

Domestic Violence Officers

- The DVOs interviewed were extremely committed to their work and offered a great deal of long-term support to the victims with whom they came into contact - including taking them to court; advising them about their civil and criminal rights; and referring them on to specialist agencies.

- DVOs appeared to have a limited impact on the *generalist* police response as they were somewhat marginalised with the force and had little to do with their uniformed colleagues. This often meant that the DVO was not kept fully informed of domestic violence incidents in her area.

- DVOs were often severely over-worked, particularly those who worked alone. Laborious referral and recording systems exacerbated this problem.

- Those DVOs who worked within Family Protection Units, whilst benefiting from the facilities available to them (interviewing rooms, comfort suites etc.), often felt that their work had a lower priority than child protection work.

- The majority of DVOs felt that they had developed good working relationships with other agencies in their area.

Victims

- Victims' contact with DVOs was described in very positive terms and it was obvious that many of them had received a great deal of support and help from a DVO.

- But victims' experiences of uniformed police were very mixed and suggest that there is still a lot of room for improvement. A sympathetic and understanding approach from the police appeared to be almost as important to the victims as whether or not their assailant was arrested.

- The way in which the courts dealt with domestic violence cases infuriated many of the victims who felt that their experience was not taken seriously.

Other agencies

- Most other agencies thought that the police had increased their awareness of domestic violence issues and had developed good policies to police such incidents. However, they were less convinced that these policies were reflected in practice – of which they were often critical.

- DVOs were seen to have improved liaison between the police and other agencies, but not as having had any impact on the general police response.

- Most respondents saw inter-agency forums as helping to develop a consistent approach to dealing with domestic violence.

Conclusions

- More attention needs to be paid to converting policies into practice, with regular training and refresher courses and systematic monitoring to ensure that cases are dealt with properly.

- The way in which domestic violence cases are recorded should be improved to enable speedy retrieval of information for officers attending incidents. This would also assist in the monitoring of domestic violence cases to enable us to obtain a better picture of the extent of the problem.

- More emphasis needs to be placed on arresting, charging and prosecuting domestic violence offenders. A more sympathetic approach to victims could increase the number willing to support police actions.

- All forces, and all divisions with those forces, should appoint at least one DVO to ensure consistent and effective support for domestic violence victims. Consideration may need to be given to the appropriateness of placing such officers within an FPU.

- DVOs need to be in frequent contact with their uniformed officers in order to have an impact upon the general police response. DVOs running training courses for uniformed officers would assist this process.

- Effective inter-agency co-operation still requires attention and all forces should consider the development of both inter-agency forums and joint training.

POLICING DOMESTIC VIOLENCE IN THE 1990s

1 Introduction

Background to the research

Over 120 women were killed by their partners or ex-partners in 1991[1] (Digest 2, 1993). In the same year, according to the British Crime Survey (BCS), there were a minimum of 530,000 incidents of domestic violence in England and Wales, 80 per cent of which involved female victims (Mayhew et al, 1992). This represents 20 per cent of all BCS violent incidents. We also know that a minimum of ten per cent of women had experienced some form of domestic violence at some time in their lives.[2]

These figures alone emphasise the importance of the police providing an effective and efficient response to domestic violence. However, the 1980s saw a string of studies criticising the police response to such incidents (see for example, Edwards, 1986 and 1989; Hamner et al, 1989; Pahl, 1985; and, for a comprehensive review of the literature, Smith, 1989 and, more recently, Morley and Mullender, 1994). The main criticism levelled at the police was that they saw domestic violence as a civil matter rather than a criminal one. Domestic violence was seen by officers as uninteresting and unexciting, ranking alongside "lost dogs...rowdy youth and bothersome drunks" (Southgate, 1986).

The police were said to be reluctant to become involved in "domestics" and to be slow to respond to such calls. When they did arrive they were said to attempt reconciliation or even side with the aggressor and assailants were rarely arrested even in cases of serious injury. In addition, a lack of adequate recording of cases of domestic violence meant that a true picture of domestic violence could not be obtained (Edwards, 1986).

The need to improve the police response to domestic assault was recognised by the police themselves and the Home Office. One aspect of the Home Office response was to recommend that procedures used to help victims of sexual assault should also apply to domestic violence victims (Home Office circular 69/1986). A second Circular (60/1990) was devoted to the policing of domestic violence. Amongst its recommendations were that the police should develop their policy and practice to take a more interventionist approach to policing domestic violence. This involved a presumption in favour of arrest where an offence had been committed; and emphasised the need to record and investigate 'domestic' offences in the same way as other violent crimes. Protecting the victim from the immediate threat of further violence was to be given priority over attempting to reconcile the victim and perpetrator; and this protection together with support for the victim was to continue throughout the criminal justice process. Forces were encouraged to set up dedicated units to deal with domestic violence or to appoint liaison officers with a particular responsibility for this offence. It was also suggested that

---

[1] This is in comparison to 30 men killed by their partners in the same year.
[2] This estimate is derived from further analysis of the 1992 British Crime Survey (Mirrlees-Black, 1994).

forces liaise with the relevant statutory and voluntary agencies to ensure a collective and united response to domestic violence.

This study examines how far these recommendations are now reflected in current force policies on domestic violence and the extent to which day-to-day police responses are affected by such policies. It began in September 1992 allowing a two year "bedding-in" period for Home Office circular 60/1990. The research focused on four main questions:

- to what extent have forces introduced new policies to deal with incidents of domestic violence?

- how do policies vary between forces?

- how successful are different approaches to dealing with domestic violence when measured in terms of "customer satisfaction"?

- which of the approaches adopted by different forces seems to be the best model?

Methodology

The first phase of the research comprised a telephone survey of all forces in England and Wales to obtain a national overview of their arrangements and policies for the policing of domestic violence. On the basis of the survey results, five forces were selected to represent a range of different approaches to dealing with domestic violence and a mixture of urban and rural areas. All five of the forces had made some moves towards dealing with domestic violence and were chosen with a view to identifying good practice.

In the second phase, semi-structured interviews were conducted in all five areas with officers of different ranks in order to see both how policy change was organised at a management level and how this affected the attitudes and practice of operational officers on a day-to-day basis. Officers specialising in domestic violence were also interviewed to obtain information about their attitudes and working practices and to compare these with those of the non-specialist officers. The interviews also explored the nature of the working relationships between the two groups. In addition, the domestic violence officers (DVOs) were observed organising their work, in particular, their record-keeping and their liaison with victims of domestic violence and with other agencies.

Interviews were also conducted with victims. These focused on their contact with the police and the criminal justice system and, in order to avoid undue distress, only touched on their experiences of domestic violence in so far as this was relevant to such contact. The interviews focused on a checklist of topics to be covered rather than taking the form of a highly structured questionnaire so that respondents were able to tell their story in their own words.

Unstructured interviews were also held with representatives from other relevant voluntary and statutory agencies - including Victim Support; Women's Aid; the Crown

Prosecution Service (CPS); Local Housing Authorities; Social Services; and any other agency which had an involvement in a particular force area. These agencies were asked about their working relationship with the police and their views on police policy and practice in relation to domestic violence.

Finally, in so far as police records allowed, levels of no-criming, cautioning and prosecution were examined in all five areas.

The shape of the report

Chapter Two outlines the findings of the telephone survey and gives a description of each of the five forces chosen to be studied in detail. Chapter Three reports the findings of the record analysis. Chapter Four compares the results of the interviews with managers and operational officers, and the work of the DVO is described in Chapter Five. In Chapter Six, the views of the victims of domestic violence are discussed. In Chapter Seven, the opinions of other agencies concerning the police response to domestic violence are reported. Overall conclusions and ideas for good practice are considered in Chapter Eight.

A note on terminology and definitions

For the purposes of this research "domestic violence" is defined as any form of physical, sexual or emotional abuse which takes place within the context of a close relationship.[3] We took "close relationship" to mean a sexual relationship and included in this ex-husbands, ex-partners and ex-boyfriends. Whilst we did not purposefully exclude homosexual relationships or heterosexual relationships where the woman is the aggressor; we made the assumption in our interviews and discussions that, in the vast majority of cases, a man will be the perpetrator and a woman the victim.[4]

---

[3] Following the definition used by the Home Affairs Select Committee on domestic violence which reported in February 1993.
[4] The term "survivor" is often now used by pressure groups (e.g. Women's Aid) and in literature (e.g. Dobash and Dobash, 1992) in the context of domestic violence. This is because of the unfavourable connotations (weakness, helplessness) associated with the term "victim". However, as this research focused on the police response to domestic violence as a crime and women as victims of that crime, it was decided that using the term survivor would not be helpful.

POLICING DOMESTIC VIOLENCE IN THE 1990s

2 The national survey and characteristics of the five sample forces

The telephone survey

All 43 police forces in England and Wales were contacted in September 1992 and asked to take part in a telephone survey. All but one force agreed. Basic information was gathered on each force's provisions for dealing with domestic violence including force policies, the existence of specialist units, record-keeping procedures, victim liaison, levels of inter-agency co-operation and training.

Policy on domestic violence

At the time of the survey, all but three forces had prepared a force policy document on domestic violence. The majority of forces had prepared their policy in response to the Home Office circular 60/1990 but in eight the policy pre-dated the Circular and in ten the policy had only been *amended* in the light of the Circular's recommendations.

Specialist units and officers

The duties of a domestic violence unit (DVU) or the domestic violence officer (DVO) are to offer support and assistance to the victim through the criminal justice process and refer her on to other agencies who can help her with any specific problems she might have. Just over half the forces had a specialist unit which had some responsibility for domestic violence but only five had domestic violence units (DVUs) dedicated solely to this offence.

Family or Child Protection Units (FPU/CPU) were more common than DVUs but in most cases these units had only a monitoring or record-keeping role in relation to domestic violence and priority was always given to child protection work. Two-thirds of those forces (n=25) without domestic violence units had a liaison officer with some degree of responsibility for domestic violence. Again, this was sometimes purely a monitoring or record keeping role but in other forces the liaison officers worked in the same way as an officer in a DVU - actively supporting victims of domestic violence.

Record keeping

Thirty-three forces felt they had an adequate system for recording and monitoring incidents of domestic violence. All but one of those who were not satisfied with their schemes planned to develop new systems. There were some who considered their manual system (card indexes, domestic violence registers etc.) as adequate but with room for improvement. The majority had, or wished to have, a system which would allow for domestic violence incidents to be automatically "flagged up" on the Command and Control computers. However, several respondents voiced uncertainties about how efficient such systems were in differentiating domestic violence from other types of assault.

Keeping the victim informed

Most forces had produced an information leaflet for victims of domestic violence but in some cases these had been prepared by other agencies, such as Victim Support, or were only available in certain divisions. Generally, those forces without leaflets were planning to produce them shortly.

Special arrangements for notifying victims of domestic violence of court dates and outcomes were rare. In a few cases, a victim or witness liaison officer had been appointed but generally it was the officer who attended the incident, or the DVO, who was responsible for keeping the victim up to date on the progress of a case. The procedures for notifying victims of the release of an offender from custody were less well established, mainly because the police were not usually notified by a prison of an offender's release date. Fifteen forces had developed a way of obtaining this information with the prisons in their area.

Inter-agency co-operation

All but two forces said they co-operated with Women's Aid, Victim Support schemes and Social Services, mainly by referring victims to them. Forces also used various local agencies which had developed an interest in the area. On the other hand, only a few forces were actively involved with inter-agency groups on domestic violence despite the Circular's recommendations that the development of such groups should be considered.

Training

Only a few respondents thought the amount of training available on domestic violence was inadequate. In general it appeared that training was limited to an element of the basic police training course. In some forces, refresher and development courses included domestic violence as one of the topics covered. Training for DVOs was provided by half of the forces with specialist officers. The need for such training was under review in three forces. Twelve forces provided aide-memoire cards on domestic violence, listing their police powers and procedures and the rights of the victims, for all their officers. Six others had plans to do so.

The five forces selected

Northamptonshire, Nottinghamshire, Thames Valley, South Yorkshire and the West Midlands were the forces selected for more detailed study. They were chosen because they represented a range of different approaches to dealing with domestic violence. This section gives a brief description of each of the forces and their arrangements for dealing with domestic violence.

THE NATIONAL SURVEY AND CHARACTERISTICS OF THE FIVE SAMPLE FORCES

Northamptonshire

Northamptonshire is a small county force covering a population of just over half a million people. It is divided into six areas or divisions. Northamptonshire devised its policy on domestic violence in 1991. A Chief Inspector at headquarters has a policy responsibility for both child protection and domestic violence, although the former takes up considerably more of his time. The decision whether to appoint DVOs was made at divisional, rather than force, level.

At the time of the study, three divisions had FPUs with a DVO - Western Favell, Wellinborough and Corby. These DVOs worked purely on domestic violence cases, and were not involved in any child protection work. They also had separate line management from the child protection officers. These three divisions were selected to take part in the research, as was a fourth division - Daventry - which had a part-time DVO, who was also the Custody Sergeant. No-one regarded this as a satisfactory arrangement, as the officer had to be in the station at all times when on duty and was not therefore able to visit victims anywhere away from the station. Nor could he accompany any victims to court.

The two Northamptonshire divisions not included in the study - Kettering and Campbell Square - did not have DVOs, but both had Detective Inspectors with responsibility for *monitoring* domestic violence cases but with no active involvement in them.

The record collection system in the three divisions with DVOs was well developed. Domestic violence referrals forms were passed on to the DVO who transferred the information onto computer. (The other four forces examined in this part of the research did not have computerised information systems.)

There was no force-wide inter-agency group on domestic violence - but there were inter-agency groups in some of the divisions.

Nottinghamshire

The Nottinghamshire force covers a population of just over a million people. Two stations in two of Nottinghamshire's four divisions were selected for study - two in Nottingham (B division) - Radford Road and Oxclose Lane; and two in rural areas - Mansfield and Worksop (A division). The force policy on domestic violence was produced in 1991. It includes a system of re-visiting victims of domestic violence 24 hours after the initial incident to ensure that the victim is no longer in danger.

Nottinghamshire has a reputation for being at the forefront of work in domestic violence mainly because of its inter-agency group (which was developed by the county council). Given this, it is perhaps surprising then that the force does not have either DVUs or DVOs.[1] However, it does have Detective Inspectors in each division with a liaison and monitoring responsibility for domestic violence cases. This appears, in most cases, to be a more active role than in other forces such as Northamptonshire. Radford Road has a civilian domestic violence worker attached to the station who fulfils some aspects of the

---

[1] Nottinghamshire has a large Child Protection Unit with over 40 staff. This covers the whole force area, working from one location.. It has no responsibility for domestic violence.

DVO role. A Chief Inspector at headquarters oversees domestic violence issues and attends the inter-agency group.

The recording of domestic violence cases is done manually through a domestic violence register[2]- completed by the investigating officer – backed up by a card index of names and addresses of victims and suspects. One duty of the Detective Inspectors with responsibility for domestic violence is to check the register regularly and chase up missing information and any entries incorrectly completed.

Thames Valley

Thames Valley force polices a large area covering parts of three counties and a population of nearly two million. Of its six divisions, three – Reading, Slough and Newbury were selected for the study[3]. The force policy was produced in 1991. Like Nottinghamshire, Thames Valley had no DVOs, however, there is a large well-established FPU based in Reading but with officers out-posted around the force. This unit has responsibility for monitoring the processing of domestic violence cases but in practice it focuses on rape and child abuse. The FPU does not carry out any active support work for victims of domestic violence. The emphasis on sexual offences may reflect the fact that it was set up in response to a television programme in 1982 which criticised Thames Valley for its treatment of rape victims.

There is a Superintendent at headquarters with a family protection remit. Shortly after the domestic violence policy was introduced an application was made at headquarters to appoint DVOs, but a decision on this was on hold at the time of the research (1992/3). There were no inter-agency groups on domestic violence in the force.

South Yorkshire

South Yorkshire's policy on domestic violence was produced in 1991. The force has jurisdiction over several large towns and cities and a population of nearly one and a half million. Four of its six divisions were chosen to be included in the study - Sheffield North and Sheffield South, Barnsley and Rotherham. All but the first of these divisions have DVOs. In Barnsley and Rotherham, the DVOs have a general victim liaison role (for victims of all offences) but most of their work is done with domestic violence victims. There are no domestic violence referral forms, but a computerised system for recording and monitoring such cases is being developed.

South Yorkshire has two large Child Protection Units (CPU) - one covering Sheffield and one for the rest of the force. These have a responsibility for recording and monitoring domestic violence cases. A Sergeant in the main CPU chairs the South Yorkshire domestic violence inter-agency group. Individual inter-agency groups, in each of the divisions with a DVO, send representatives to the main group.

---

[2] This contains basic details about the incident - names and addresses of the parties involved; allegations made; police action taken; and is updated as the case progresses.

[3] Both Milton Keynes and Oxford were considered for inclusion but another project on domestic violence was being conducted in these areas. To avoid undue pressure on the force, these areas were excluded from the current study.

No senior officer at headquarters has a specific responsibility for overseeing domestic violence matters – this is left to the Sergeant in the main CPU. The force is presently looking at the possibility of piloting a civilian crisis intervention team to deal with domestic violence incidents.

West Midlands

This is a large metropolitan force covering a population of over two and a half million people. It has 11 divisions (excluding traffic and headquarters). Two inner city divisions were chosen –"B" and "C" and two "outer" divisions – Dudley and Coventry. Each division in the West Midlands has at least one DVO – often attached to a Family Protection Unit (FPU). Those officers who are attached to an FPU share line management with the child protection officers, in that they are directly answerable to the Sergeant in charge of the FPU.

The force policy was produced in 1991. There is no force-wide inter-agency group – as officers felt that the force was too large for this to be useful. Instead, local groups in most of the divisions have been developed. There is an Inspector at headquarters with responsibility solely for domestic violence policy and practice. She does not get involved in child protection issues.

The record collection system is manual and cumbersome. Most DVOs have devised their own referral forms for uniformed officers to complete after attending an incident and pass to the DVO for recording in a card index. At the end of each day, the DVOs take their card index to the Command and Control room (so that the information is available outside of office hours) and collect them again the following morning. The possibility of computerising this process is being explored.

POLICING DOMESTIC VIOLENCE IN THE 1990s

3 Analysis of the processing of domestic violence cases

Introduction

Home Office circular 60/1990 encouraged the police to record cases of domestic violence; to arrest domestic violence offenders whenever appropriate; and, as for any other violent assault, to charge such offenders. One of the aims of this research was to assess how far the police were following that advice.

Although it would have been useful to examine the processing of domestic violence cases pre- and post-circular, obtaining any data on domestic violence cases from police records prior to 1991 (when the Circular was issued) was impossible, as such cases were not recorded separately from other violent incidents then. We therefore focused on "post-circular" practice and collected a sample of cases from the third quarter of 1992. Thus each force had one year, from issue of the Circular, to implement a process for systematically recording domestic violence cases.

The records sample was taken from the same divisions in each force as the interviewing sample. Data were collected in two stages: first, information on the initial incident reported to the police, including whether an arrest was made; and second, action taken by the police in those cases resulting in an arrest.

Initially, our police contacts in each area were reasonably confident that 1992 data would be available. However, the quality and the sources of this information varied considerably from force to force. The results discussed in this chapter should therefore be treated with caution. What the results do show very clearly is that systematic recording of domestic violence cases was still lacking in all but one of the areas studied.

The only clear exception to this in the current study was the West Midlands where domestic violence cases are coded separately on a computerised Command and Control system. We were therefore able to obtain information on virtually all domestic violence incidents reported to the police there during the selected time period, although some more serious cases of domestic violence might have been coded as GBH. Despite this, of the five forces examined, the West Midlands system provides the most reliable information on the incidence of domestic violence reported to the police. Cases where an arrest was made were followed up using DVO's records supplemented, where necessary, by Administrative Support Unit (ASU) records.

Data on domestic violence incidents were also held on the Command and Control system in Thames Valley. However, it was not possible to link information about individual cases on the Command and Control system with information about charging and prosecution decisions. In order to obtain an estimate of charge rates, we took a separate sample of one month's cases from one station's custody records and followed these through to the charge stage.

Initial incident information in Nottinghamshire was collected from the domestic violence registers in which officers are expected to record the details of each domestic violence incident they attend and of any follow up work conducted. Cases were traced through to the charging stage using ASU and custody records. In Northamptonshire we used forms ("Dom1s") completed by officers attending domestic violence incidents as our basic source of information. Most of the information on the charging of offenders was also taken from this source, again supplemented by ASU data where necessary.

Information on initial incidents from Nottinghamshire and Northamptonshire was less satisfactory than that taken from Command and Control computer systems as domestic violence registers and Dom1 forms are not always completed.[1]

South Yorkshire were unable to provide us with any initial incident information as they had not, by the third quarter of 1992, implemented any systematic way of separately recording domestic violence cases. We therefore took a one month sample of cases from one station's custody records to follow through to charge.

The results

Initial incidents

Initial incident information was only satisfactory for the West Midlands and Thames Valley forces. These data showed that there were 2,016 domestic violence incidents which occurred during July, August and September 1992. Of these, 1,505 occurred in the West Midlands and 511 in Thames Valley.

Information on sex and the victim-suspect relationship was only available for the West Midlands. The sex of the suspect was available for 93 per cent of cases.[2] Of these 97 per cent involved male suspects and female victims. We have no way of knowing how far the three per cent of cases involving female suspects and male victims represent the real proportion of such cases. Information on the relationship between the victim and the suspect was available in 85 per cent of cases (n=1272). The largest group comprised husbands and wives (39 per cent) with a further eight per cent involving ex-husbands and wives. Sixteen per cent of cases involved common-law husbands and wives; and three per cent of cases concerned ex-common-law husbands and wives. Seventeen per cent and 15 per cent of cases involved boyfriends and girlfriends and ex-boyfriends and girlfriends respectively.[3]

Twelve per cent of incidents initially recorded as domestic violence in the West Midlands resulted in an arrest, as did 14 per cent of those in Thames Valley.[4]

---

[1] Our interviews with both general police officers and DVOs reinforced this finding.
[2] In the seven per cent of cases where information was missing, it was unclear who was the victim and who was the suspect. Such cases tended to involve "couple fighting next door" reports.
[3] The definition of boyfriend and girlfriend were a couple who were not living together. The remaining two per cent of cases involved "other" relationships.
[4] Arrest rates for the other areas are not presented here because of doubts about the completeness of data on initial incidents.

ANALYSIS OF THE PROCESSING OF DOMESTIC VIOLENCE CASES

Information on whether the suspects arrested were subject to an injunction order against them was only available for the West Midlands cases. There were only 50 cases (three per cent) in which we could be certain that the victim had taken out an injunction order against the assailant. Of these injunctions, nine had powers of arrest attached to them. Similarly, information on whether the suspect had been arrested on a previous occasion for domestic violence was only available for the West Midlands and in only 51 cases were we able to establish that there had been such an arrest.

In the 1,505 cases in the West Midlands[5] all but 12 per cent of cases were dealt with at the scene and recorded as "no further police action". However, the "no further action" tag should not be taken entirely at face value. In 43 per cent of these cases the incident was recorded as having been sent to the DVU for information and in 37 per cent either, or both, the victim and the suspect were advised by the police (we do not of course know the nature of that advice).[6]

Charge

Information on further proceedings by the police was available for 318 of the 328 suspects arrested in the West Midlands, Nottinghamshire and Northamptonshire. Of these 81 per cent were charged; five per cent (n=7) were cautioned; and one per cent (n=3) were summoned. All but two per cent of the remaining 13 per cent of cases were coded as being dealt with in an "other" way. These comprised those cases where the complaint was withdrawn and/or a decision was made to release the suspect without charge. A further six cases were described as not proceeding to charge due to insufficient evidence (in five cases) and "public interest" (in one case) and one case was described as being dealt by way of an informal warning.

The special data collection exercise in both Thames Valley and South Yorkshire showed that 60 per cent of the 63 arrest cases in both areas resulted in a charge being laid; in five cases there was no further action due to insufficient evidence; and three suspects were cautioned. The suspects in the remaining 14 cases were released without charge – generally because the Custody Sergeant refused the charge due to lack of evidence.[7]

Table 3.1 shows the *types* of offences with which suspects were charged. It can be seen that the most commonly used charged was ABH (actual bodily harm). For ease of reference, percentages are used, but it is important to bear in mind the small numbers used in the Thames Valley (n=38) and South Yorkshire (n=25) samples.

---

[5] This information was not available for Thames Valley.
[6] In just under half of these "advice only" cases, no complaint had been made and/or no offences had been disclosed.
[7] Information was not available for three cases.

Table 3.1 - Types of offences with which suspects were charged

	Main Sample* %	Thames Valley %	South Yorkshire %
GBH (Section 18)	2	-	-
GBH (Section 20)	3	5	5
ABH	43	27	45
Common Assault	4	5	-
Criminal damage	7	23	-
Breach of the Peace	25	9	25
Other[8]	16	31	25
	(n=256)	(n=38)	(n=25)

* West Midlands, Nottinghamshire and Northamptonshire

A small number of suspects were charged with more than one offence (n=52). The second charge was normally less serious than the first and was most commonly common assault or criminal damage.

Key points

These results suggest an arrest rate in domestic violence cases of between 12 and 14 per cent, leading to a charge rate of 81 per cent. They also suggest that most suspects were charged with ABH if they were charged at all. However, problems of collecting information on domestic violence incidents mean that these figures should be treated with caution. Until there is systematic recording of such cases across *all* forces, the results described in this chapter can only be used with a great degree of circumspection.

---

[8] The "other" charges were many and various. Most frequent were breach of bail conditions (n=12); public order offences (n=12); drunk and disorderly (n=6); and breach of injunction (n=5). Other less frequent charges included burglary, theft, possession of an offensive weapon, perverting the course of justice, breach of a bind over, unlawful entry, buggery and affray.

4 The response to domestic violence from operational officers and their managers

In this chapter, the results of interviews with both *operational* police officers and their *managers*[1] are discussed. The interviews were similar in that both groups were asked about policing domestic violence in practice and the extent to which they knew about and were affected by policy changes. However, the interviews differed in that managers were asked more detailed questions about any new initiatives on domestic violence and the implementation of policy, whereas the operational officers were asked more about dealing with domestic violence cases on a day-to-day basis.

The interview samples

Managers ranged in rank from Sergeant to Superintendent. Half of them were 31 to 40 years of age; the rest were over 40 years of age. Thirty-one were men and six were women. Officers had served between six and 30 years in the police and all were serving in their current force before 1990 (that is before Home Office circular 60/1990 had been issued).

One hundred and one operational officers were interviewed[2] of whom 66 were Constables; 22 were probationers (that is in their first two years of service); and 13 were Sergeants. All of them were from the uniformed branch of the forces and none were domestic violence specialists.

Two-thirds of the operational officers had been serving in their force before 1990; a third had not joined the police prior to 1990; and one officer had been serving in a different force. Half had served less than four years and three-quarters had served less than nine. Of the remaining quarter, 12 officers had served over 15 years.

Changes in policing domestic violence

All but one of the managers[3] thought that the policing of domestic violence had changed since they had joined the police. Two-thirds of operational officers agreed, with equal proportions of the remainder saying that they had "grown up" with the changes introduced, having only been in the service a relatively short time; or that there simply had not been any changes, mainly because new policies had confirmed existing practice.

Most of the managers and the operational officers who felt that changes had occurred, thought that the majority of their colleagues took domestic violence more seriously - by arresting offenders more often and by getting involved in cases rather than just giving advice at the scene or attempting reconciliation. Other changes mentioned, particularly by operational officers, included being more sympathetic to victims and conducting more

---

[1] The operational officers were Constables and Sergeants in the uniformed branches who dealt with domestic violence cases on a day-to-day basis. The officers included in the management sample had line management responsibility for operational officers or for DVOs who dealt directly with domestic violence victims and perpetrators.
[2] We had intended to interview 20 officers per force but an overzealous researcher conducted an extra interview in South Yorkshire - giving a total sample of 101.
[3] The remaining officer thought that the new policies had simply confirmed the existing practice of arresting and prosecuting offenders.

follow-up, support work with them; being more aware of the long-term nature of most domestic violence; having clearer guidelines on exactly how to deal with domestic violence cases; the introduction of DVOs and DVUs; and proper recording of domestic violence incidents. They talked about how changes in the police culture had made it easier to take domestic violence seriously, without being ridiculed by their colleagues (which they said had sometimes happened in the past). Several of the managers commented that having a set policy had made dealing with domestic violence more straightforward as, in the past, they had been unsure how to police it. Many interviewees said that younger officers might find it easier to take the new guidelines into account as they were not so set in their ways.

Impact of the Circular

Two-thirds (n=66) of the operational officers said that they had heard of Home Office circular 60/1990, but 20 were unclear about what it had said. A third said that they had not heard of the Circular at all. Only two of the managers said this. Most of those officers who had heard of the Circular said that there had been some changes in the way domestic violence was policed in their force since it had been issued. Managers were generally better able to specify what those changes had been, but most officers mentioned new force guidance on domestic violence, and the setting up of DVUs or the appointment of DVOs. Fewer mentioned systems for recording domestic violence incidents. Less than half of the operational officers said that they had personally received any new guidelines on how to deal with domestic violence. This is despite the fact that, when asked about implementing new initiatives, most managers mentioned briefing uniformed shifts and passing round guidelines.

Implementing new guidelines on domestic violence

All thirty-seven managers were questioned in some depth about changes in policy and practice for domestic violence and any problems which had arisen. Thirty mentioned organisational changes which had come about as a result of the new initiatives which mainly involved setting up a DVU or adding domestic violence to the responsibilities of the FPU. Seven managers said there had been no organisational changes to facilitate new policies on domestic violence.

As the Circular had stressed the importance of monitoring domestic violence cases, managers were asked about such arrangements. Most said that domestic violence incidents were now recorded on a special domestic violence proforma, in a register or on a card index. Managers said that these records were then sometimes monitored by the DVOs and the results were sometimes reported to their line management.

When asked whether they had been hampered in any way from fully implementing new guidelines, a lack of resources was mentioned by 21 managers, time by 18 and the attitude of operational officers and managers by ten and six respectively.

Other constraints mentioned by individual respondents included the attitudes of the CPS towards prosecuting domestic violence cases; insufficient evidence to take cases forward to prosecution; lack of computer support for the proper recording of domestic violence incidents; and being "victims of their own success" (i.e. DVOs becoming more and more busy). Some officers also mentioned a lack of knowledge about what other agencies can do; a lack of training; and a lack of proper help for the offender.

Policing domestic violence and policing other assaults

Home Office circular 60/1990 stated that "a violent assault in a domestic situation should be treated as seriously as a violent assault by a stranger". Around two-thirds of the managers and operational officers interviewed saw policing domestic violence as a different job to policing other violent crimes, because the intimate relationship between the victim and the offender and the emotional context in which the violence occurred made domestic violence incidents far more complex. The long history that usually came before any particular domestic assault was also said to complicate matters and officers felt that any action they might take could have a profound effect on the couple involved:

> *".....it's not so straightforward. There's a lengthy background to the incident we're called to, it's never clear cut. And there are always difficulties after the event...."*

Most of the other interviewees thought that policing domestic violence was the same kind of job as policing any other violent crime:

> *"I don't think you can draw a distinction - ABH is ABH and at the end of the day it's [domestic violence] still as much an offence".*

But 11 operational officers said that whether policing domestic violence was the same or different to policing other violent crime depended on circumstances - particularly the degree of violence used and the seriousness of the injury sustained.

Half of the managers (n=19) thought that policing domestic violence had the same priority as other types of violent crime for their forces. Ten said that it had a higher priority and seven that it had a lower priority than other types of violent crime.

The need for domestic violence officers

Just over half of the managers (n=20) and 42 per cent of their operational colleagues thought that a combination of uniformed officers dealing with initial incidents and DVOs conducting any follow-up work was the best system for dealing with domestic violence cases. The same proportion of operational officers and seven managers saw no particular need for specialist domestic violence officers, whereas ten managers and 18 operational officers thought that DVOs should have the main responsibility for domestic violence cases.

Officers in both groups who had no experience of working with DVOs saw little value in having specialist teams, but these officers also appeared to misunderstand what DVOs do, saying that as DVOs were not available 24 hours a day, they would not be available to help police most domestic violence incidents. In fact what the Circular actually recommends is that DVOs should offer follow-up support rather than respond to initial incidents.

Most respondents thought that DVOs should have a combination of counselling skills – compassion, being a good listener – and knowledge about legislation and procedures in domestic violence. Operational officers mentioned "patience" more frequently. We cannot be certain why this is, but it may suggest that they, themselves, may find dealing with such cases frustrating.

Most officers said that it was better to have a mixture of men and women specialising in domestic violence. However, more managers favoured having female DVOs (25 per cent as opposed to 12 per cent of the operational officers).

Relations with domestic violence officers

Fifty-six of the operational officers worked in a station which had a domestic violence officer.[4] Over half of these (n=29) described their relationship with the DVO as "good"; 19 described it as "reasonable"; and seven either said they did not feel that they had enough personal contact with the DVO to make a judgement or did not express any opinion. Those who described the relationship as "good" were generally those officers who had the most personal contact with the DVOs. Officers said they particularly appreciated being kept in touch by DVOs about the progress and outcome of cases in which they had attended the initial incident.

Checking records for previous incidents

Home Office circular 60/1990 recommended that records of domestic violence incidents "should be kept in a manner which permits easy information retrieval so that officers dispatched to an incident can readily establish where there have been previous reports on the household, their frequency and the nature of previous threats of violence". Managers were asked whether officers could do this in practice. Most (n=29) thought that it would be possible, of whom three said that it would depend on whether there was sufficient time to do so.

Only a quarter of operational officers (n=25) stated that they were *always* able to check their records before attending a domestic violence incident to find out what had happened in the past. A further twenty said they were able to do so - time permitting. The majority of these officers said that they would obtain this information from the Control Room, but that often the Controller was too busy to give them the information *before* they attended the incident. In several stations, the Controller had to ring through to the DVO to obtain background information, making it less likely that the officer would receive the information before attending the incident.

Over half of the operational officers, compared to only eight of the 37 managers, said that they either could not or did not check records in this way. Many of these officers

---

[4] None of the 40 officers interviewed in Thames Valley and Nottinghamshire had contact with the domestic violence officers and five of the officers from South Yorkshire worked in a station without a domestic violence officer (Sheffield North).

said that their priority was to get to the incident as soon as possible and that checking records only held them up. A quarter of operational officers said they would rely more on their local knowledge of the area and of "domestic violence families" and would often already know the people they were going to see. In contrast, some officers said they preferred to go in with an open mind and not be influenced about what had happened in the past - an approach which would appear to go directly against the recommendations of the Circular. Sixteen officers said that they would check up on records after the event, when they had more time to find out what had gone on in the past.

Most managers and operational officers said that it was possible to check whether there was a civil injunction in place (for example to prevent the victim's partner coming to her home). Some operational officers (n=12) said that this depended on whether the solicitor who had obtained the injunction sent a copy of it to the Control Room. Twenty operational officers said they could not check for injunction information.

Police powers in respect of domestic violence incidents

Home Office circular 60/1990 suggested that officers should be fully aware of their powers in respect of domestic violence and pointed out that these were extensive.

Table 4.1 Types of police powers mentioned by officers [5]

Power	Managers	Operational
	No.	No.
Breach of the Peace	32	95
Offences against the person	27	73
PACE Powers to enter for purposes of making an arrest	9	19
Common Assault	8	37
Criminal Damage	5	17
Breach of injunction or court order	5	15
Public Order	4	22
Threats to kill	2	
Total	37	101

As Table 4.1 shows, a majority of managers and operational officers said that domestic violence was commonly dealt with either as a Breach of the Peace or under the Offences Against the Person Act (1861). In discussing how they decided which powers to use with operational officers it became apparent that using any power but Breach of the Peace was exceptional (perhaps because Breach of the Peace does not require the complainant's support). Indeed, officers sometimes described using this power even in very violent circumstances. In fact one operational officer said to the researcher that one domestic violence incident he had attended "was the most violent Breach of the Peace that [he'd] ever seen"!

---

[5] Officers could give more than one response. Thus the numbers in this table and in subsequent tables in this and the next chapter do not necessarily add up to the total number of officers interviewed.

POLICING DOMESTIC VIOLENCE IN THE 1990s

Priorities at the scene

The Home Office circular suggested that reconciliation is rarely the most appropriate solution to domestic violence and that what victims require is enforcement of the law and "the arrest and detention of the alleged assailant should [therefore] always be considered". Three-quarters of the operational officers (n=77) said that if the perpetrator was still at the scene when they arrived at an incident, or if there had only been a verbal dispute, they would attempt to cool down the situation without necessarily making an arrest. Two-thirds of the managers said that they supported this approach. Both groups said that the action taken would and should depend on certain circumstances – in particular how violent the situation was and whether there were any obvious injuries. Many managers said that if the situation was relatively calm, officers should at least try to get the couple to discuss what had happened before deciding whether an arrest was appropriate. Operational officers said that if it seemed as though they would not have enough medical evidence to prove that an assault had taken place they were more inclined to deal with the incident informally, without making an arrest. Sixteen operational officers also mentioned that they would take what the complainant wanted into account when deciding whether to make an arrest.

Fifteen operational officers said they would always try to cool things down without making an arrest and seven managers agreed that this was the correct course of action. Only nine of the operational officers said that they would not attempt mediation.

Officers were asked to say which of the following aims should be given priority at a domestic violence incident: calming the situation down; arresting the offender; the safety of the victim; and the safety of her children. A fifth aim was subsequently created, combining the safety of the victim and the children, as many officers found it difficult to separate the two factors.[6]

---

[6] The numbers in the table do not add up to the total samples as a small number of officers could not prioritise their aims and others did not choose as many as four aims.

THE RESPONSE TO DOMESTIC VIOLENCE FROM OPERATIONAL OFFICERS AND THEIR MANAGERS

Table 4.2 Operational officer's priorities at the scene of a domestic violence incident (N = 101) [7]

	safety of victim	safety of children	safety of both*	calming situation	arrest
	%	%	%	%	%
1st priority	26	16	36	17	2
2nd priority	19	29	9	34	5
3rd priority	7	5	1	39	38
4th priority	0	1	0	5	48

Table 4.3 Managers' priorities at the scene of a domestic violence incident (N = 37)

	safety of victim	safety of children	safety of both*	calming situation	arrest
	%	%	%	%	%
1st priority	43	11	22	3	3
2nd priority	19	40	–	22	5
3rd priority	3	16	–	32	40
4th priority	3	–	–	3	35

*safety of both victim and children

In line with the spirit of circular 60/1990, most managers put the safety of the victim first, followed by the safety of the victim and children combined, whereas most operational officers put the safety of both the victim and the children as their first priority followed by the safety of the victim alone. Calming down the situation and arresting the perpetrator was accorded low priority by both groups.

The Circular also suggested that officers arrange medical attention for victims if it is required and that they provide victims with basic information about the sources of help which are available to them. Managers were keen for their officers to give victims contact numbers for helpful agencies. For most operational officers this involved putting the victim in touch with the DVO or giving her an information leaflet. Table 4.4 shows the kinds of actions which officers thought might be useful to victims at the scene.

---

[7] For tables 4.2 and 4.3 percentages rather than whole numbers are used for ease of comparison. However, it should be noted that the senior officer sample only contained 37 respondents.

Table 4.4 Actions which should be considered at the scene

Action	Managers	Operational
	No.	No.
Advise the victim to see a solicitor	35	97
Give victim contact numbers for helpful agencies	34	82
Take the victim to doctor or a hospital/send for an ambulance	33	89
Take the victim to a relative	33	98
Take the victim to a refuge	27	88
Total	*37*	*101*

Problems in dealing with domestic violence cases

Some managers said that younger operational officers might find dealing with domestic violence incidents particularly difficult as they might feel "out of their depth" and unable to relate to the circumstances in which domestic violence occurs. They might also find it difficult to tell people, often many years older than them, how to "run their lives". Compounding this problem, was the feeling that domestic violence situations can be very volatile and the police officer can end up being turned on by both the offender and the victim.

A second problem was that officers felt frustrated when a victim withdrew her complaint or did not turn up at court to act as a witness. Managers thought that there was a lack of understanding on the officer's part as to why victims might do this. Three managers even speculated that some officers might beat their own partners and thus find it difficult to deal objectively with domestic violence cases. Of course, we have no way of knowing whether this is true.

Perhaps understandably, the operational officers, who were actually dealing with the incidents on a day-to-day basis, appeared in interview to be more reluctant than managers to admit that they found them problematic. At the outset, a third (n=35) admitted to experiencing difficulties in dealing with domestic violence. However as interviews proceeded many others went on to describe problems they had had. They described feeling frustrated about dealing with the same people over and over again, and thus, as they saw it, continually wasting their time. This frustration was exacerbated when victims withdrew complaints – which they described as simply adding to their paperwork load without producing tangible benefits for anyone. Because of these frustrations, officers said that they felt they were in a "no-win" situation with domestic violence cases and whatever they did they could not get it right.

Those officers who said that they did not have any problems or difficulties tended to be the older officers who felt that after years of dealing with these cases, they no longer found them a problem. It is not possible to say how far their confidence was justified but, as discussed above, both managers and operational officers had expressed doubts about how far older officers had taken new guidance into account.

THE RESPONSE TO DOMESTIC VIOLENCE FROM OPERATIONAL OFFICERS AND THEIR MANAGERS

Action after the incident

Circular 60/1990 suggested that officers should provide the CPS with as much background information as possible on domestic incidents in order to help them prosecute the case effectively. The following table shows the kind of background information operational officers considered they should be supplying to the CPS should a case go forward for prosecution.

Table 4.5 Background information for the CPS[8]

Information	No.
Previous police intervention for domestic violence	79
Nature and history of relationship (including violence)	68
Previous general offending history	59
Composition of family	37
Domestic arrangements of family (including financial)	33
Present and future status of relationship	22
Likelihood of victim withdrawing her complaint	14
Injunction information	13
Types of injuries/violence used	12

n=101 (operational officer sample)

Most officers mentioned previous police involvement and other previous evidence of violent and other offending as the sort of information they would mention to the CPS. A substantial minority said that they would also mention family composition, domestic arrangements and whether the relationship was likely to be sustained. Other factors, such as whether there were any civil proceedings taking place or whether there was an injunction in place against the offender were mentioned less often. Twenty officers said that they would provide "the same as they would for any offence".

Withdrawn complaints

When operational officers were asked about victims withdrawing complaints, less than a quarter (n=22) said that they thought most victims now withdrew their complaints, although some added that this certainly used to be the case. Fourteen were certain that the majority did not withdraw their complaints; 20 officers thought that less than half of victims withdrew; and 16 officers thought it was "about 50:50".[9]

Over half of the operational officers (n=54) said that if a victim decided to withdraw her complaint they would ask her to make a formal retraction statement so that the case could be closed officially. A third of officers (n=32) said they would try to find out why the victim did not wish to continue and a similar number said they would simply submit a report to the CPS and that it would be for them decide whether to proceed. Other actions mentioned were trying to persuade the victim of the importance of pursuing the charge; and warning her that the case may proceed without her (n=21); trying to continue the case without the victim (n=19); advising the victim about other "non-criminal"

---

[8] This table and the discussion are based on operational officers' replies, as they are more actively involved in the charging and prosecution process.
[9] The remaining five officers did not feel experienced enough to make a judgement as very few of the cases in which they had been involved had resulted in a charge or a prosecution.

options and services (n=5); and making the victim withdraw her complaint at court (n=5). Eight officers said that they would not be involved in this process as the DVO dealt with victims who wished to withdraw. Seven officers also said that they would ask the DVO to visit the victim to find out why she was withdrawing.

The results presented in Table 4.6 suggest that officers appreciated many of the problems victims faced when deciding to withdraw a complaint. They recognised that, while some women might wish to be reconciled with their partners, it was just as likely that women were too afraid of reprisals from their partner to pursue a complaint. They also mentioned the potential long-term implications for the victim of pursuing a prosecution – losing her home, breaking up the family etc. Very few officers said that they blamed victims for withdrawing a complaint.

Table 4.6 Reasons for victims withdrawing according to operational officers

Reason	No.
Still loves/wishes to be reconciled with violent partner	59
Fear of reprisal from partner	53
Fear of losing children/wanting to keep family together/need for security	31
Scared to go to court/did not want it to go that far	25
Anticipation of future problems if partner imprisoned	20
Pressure from family or friends not to proceed	10
Complaint made in the heat of the moment	7
Lack of faith in the criminal justice system	7
Violence accepted as a way of life	6
Guilt/self blame	6
Shame/embarrassment/stigma	5
Drunk when made the allegation, changed mind when sober	4
False allegation	1

n=101 (operational officer sample)

Keeping the victim informed

Circular 60/1990 emphasised the importance of offering continued support for domestic violence victims and keeping them informed of the progress of a case and in particular the whereabouts of the offender. Most of the operational officers (n=70) and over half of the managers (n=21) considered that the investigating officer should keep the victim informed. A quarter of operational officers and 14 managers said that it was the DVO's job to do this. Several officers also mentioned the role of the Administrative Support Unit (ASU) and the victim liaison officer in providing information to victims.

Information and training

Circular 60/1990 suggested that Chief Constables should ensure that all officers likely to be involved in domestic violence incidents were familiar with their powers in such cases and thoroughly understood force policies and procedures, particularly in respect of liaison with other agencies. Over three-quarters of managers thought that operational officers had access to both an information leaflet on domestic violence and a copy of force guidelines, whereas only two-thirds of operational officers said that they had access to either. Less than a third (n=31) of operational officers were able to refer to an aide-memoire card on domestic violence and only seven managers thought that their officers had been issued with such a card. Eleven managers said that they had "no idea" whether they had been issued or not. Over half of the officers felt that they could seek the advice of a DVO about how to deal with domestic violence cases and two-thirds of managers also thought they could do this. However, three of the latter were from forces which did not have DVOs!

Two-thirds of the managers (n=23) thought that special training was required to deal effectively with domestic violence, whereas less than half (n=41) of the operational officers felt that this would be useful. In fact, less than a quarter of operational officers (n=23) had received any specific training.

The officers who said that training would be beneficial suggested this should include knowledge about civil law and other options available to the victim; information on which support agencies do what; and how to refer victims to support agencies; together with training on awareness of domestic violence issues; sensitive interviewing and counselling skills. Several managers also emphasised the importance of refresher training to help reinforce the importance of dealing with such incidents properly.

Inter-agency working

Circular 60/1990 recommended that the police develop inter-agency groups with the CPS and other agencies to discuss liaison arrangements and promote understanding of force policy amongst other relevant agencies. Fifteen managers said that their force was involved in an inter-agency group for domestic violence; 13 said they were not and nine did not know.[10] Most of those that were involved in inter-agency working described the main benefits as the sharing of information, knowledge and ideas, and that it encouraged all the agencies involved to pull in the same direction. Others also said that being involved in inter-agency groups had improved the image of the police and encouraged other agencies to use them and to believe that they could and would help. Ten officers voiced some concerns about inter-agency working. These centred around agencies having different agendas and priorities – but most thought that such differences could be dealt with given time.

Key points

Most officers, both managers and operational staff, appeared to have a basic understanding of force policy. However, operational officers were both less well-informed than their managers and less well-informed than their managers thought them to be. Comparing the responses of managers and operational officers suggests that the former were somewhat optimistic about what the latter knew and did. Despite the fact that most managers said that a lot had been done to "get the message across" to the

---

[10] Most of those officers who did not know were shift inspectors and would not therefore have any direct connection with inter-agency work.

operational officers, less than half of the operational officers said that they had received any new guidelines on domestic violence and few had received any training.

All five forces' policies recommended arresting a suspect where possible or appropriate and most officers were aware of this advice. But most officers accorded arrest a low priority – almost half of the operational officers put it below all other considerations.

An officer's decision about whether to arrest and charge a perpetrator was influenced by their judgement as to whether a complainant would support any police action. One way in which officers "got round this problem" was by using Breach of the Peace, as the support of a complainant is not necessary. However, officers described using Breach of the Peace for violent cases where the victim suffered injury and therefore an arrest for Actual Bodily Harm or even Grievous Bodily Harm could have been more appropriate.

Policing domestic violence incidents within what is known in the domestic violence literature as an "historical context" [11] (Sheptycki, 1993) was another recommendation of Circular 60/1990, yet only a quarter of operational officers said that they were consistently able to check records before they attended domestic violence incidents.

There is evidence that many officers have increased their awareness about domestic violence and are more inclined to give an active response in such cases; and to show more sympathy to victims and a greater understanding about the circumstances in which domestic violence occurs.

---

11 This means that the police know about prior episodes of violence and the nature and severity of this violence, thus enabling them to consider the present incident within the context of an on-going situation.

5 Domestic violence officers

Background

One of the recommendations of Home Office circular 60/1990 was that chief officers should consider the creation of domestic violence officer (DVO) posts (if they had not already been appointed) to "perform a more active role in supporting and reassuring the victim and helping her to make reasoned decisions, and [in] coordinating the work of the welfare and voluntary agencies". The domestic violence unit (DVU) or DVO would also provide support for, and liaise with, uniformed officers dealing with domestic violence cases, and maintain up-to-date knowledge of suitable referral points for other agencies.

At the time of the study, three of the five forces examined had DVOs – West Midlands, Northamptonshire and South Yorkshire. The way in which these DVOs were assigned varied considerably. In the West Midlands, there was at least one DVO working in each of the 11 divisions but in Northamptonshire and South Yorkshire only some divisions had appointed DVOs.

Twenty-four DVOs were interviewed in total: sixteen from West Midlands, four from Northamptonshire and four from South Yorkshire. In order to get a reasonable sample of DVOs, it was decided to interview as many DVOs from the West Midlands as were available, rather than just focus on the officers working in the selected divisions. The obvious effect of this over-sampling of the West Midlands is that we have a better idea of how DVOs operated there. However, DVOs throughout all three forces shared very similar working methods and problems so the effect of having so many DVOs from one force in the sample was not strong.

Interviews with DVOs focused on their role in helping victims of domestic violence, the way in which they recorded domestic violence incidents and their relationships with both their uniformed colleagues and with other agencies. Time was also spent with the DVOs talking to them about their work, seeing the facilities available to them (interviewing rooms, comfort suites etc.), looking through their records and generally getting a feel for what their job entailed.

Of the 24 DVOs interviewed, 20 were female Constables and three were male Constables. The remaining officer was a female Sergeant. Sixteen of the officers were aged 31 to 40 years; one was older and the others younger.

The DVOs had served between four and 19 years in the police, with 17 having served over ten years. However, none of the officers had specialised in domestic violence for more than four years, with the majority serving three years or less in the field. This reflects the fact that there was a limit on the tenure of a DVO post of two, three or five years in the three forces. Most DVOs found this tenure restrictive, saying that they had only really begun to understand the complex issues of and legislation about domestic violence and had only just made good links with all the various agencies when it came time for them to move on. This was particularly true when the period of tenure was only two years.

How the DVOs operated

Thirteen of the DVOs worked in a Family Protection Unit (FPU) or a Family Support Unit (FSU) which also had responsibility for child protection work. However, most of these officers worked exclusively on domestic violence cases but shared facilities and line management with the child protection officers. Five DVOs described themselves as working in a Domestic Violence Unit (DVU) and six as working independently as domestic violence liaison officers.

DVOs themselves tended to use the terms FPU, DVU, DVO and domestic violence liaison officers interchangeably. For example, those officers who worked in an FPU sometimes described themselves as working in a DVU and those officers who worked alone still felt that they ran a DVU.

Twenty of the DVOs described their role as fully or primarily supportive, meaning that they worked almost exclusively with victims. Very few had any involvement with the investigative side of the case (arresting and interviewing the offender, giving evidence in court etc.). Most felt that this was an appropriate way to operate as they could not support the victim so actively if they were involved in the investigation. For example, if they were a witness in the case, having made an arrest, they would not be allowed to speak to the victim about the court case or go to court with her.

The majority of DVOs saw the care and protection of the victim as their main function. The other two felt it was a mixture of care and protection and the prevention of further violence. Six officers mentioned other priorities, centering around liaison with other agencies and offering continued after-care to the victim. None saw the arrest and prosecution of the suspect as a priority for them.

Training

Fourteen of the 24 DVOs had received some training in domestic violence work. The other ten had received no training at all. Ten of the 16 West Midlands DVOs had been on an introductory domestic violence officer course at the local training school. Other officers had had counselling and interviewing skills training. In addition, many officers had been to visit other DVUs and representatives of other relevant agencies at the beginning of their appointment and had found this kind of informal information-gathering very useful.

Several officers thought that training was not essential and that general experience, of life and of being a police officer, and maturity, were far more important.

When asked what kind of training they would like to receive, ten officers mentioned counselling training and sensitive interviewing techniques. Others mentioned computer skills (for keeping computer records rather than manual ones); finding out what other agencies do and gaining from their expertise; learning about the underlying causes of domestic violence; training in civil remedies; and publicity training.

Impact of the Home Office circular

All of the DVOs described themselves as either familiar or very familiar with Home Office circular 60/1990 and all but one said that it had had an influence on the way in which their force dealt with domestic violence. Nine DVOs said that the Circular had directly led to their appointment as a DVO and that its recommendations had shaped their job description. In fact, several DVOs described being simply handed the Circular on their first day and told to "get on with it". Nine officers also said that the Circular had helped to change the attitudes of the police and led to a more positive approach in dealing with domestic violence in their force and in encouraging arrest and prosecution. The officers felt that the Circular had also given clear guidelines on how to deal with domestic violence cases which had not been available previously.

The one officer who did not think the Circular had had an influence said "*It may have at headquarters, but not at street level*".

Helping the victim

All of the DVOs made direct contact with the victim – by letter, visit or telephone. Most used a mixture of these approaches. All but one of the DVOs said that they used strategies for making contact with the victim without the knowledge of the violent partner. This was done in various ways, some of which were rather haphazard. For example, letters were sent out without the force's headed note paper (but sometimes in identifiable envelopes); and, when phoning or visiting the victim, plain clothes officers pretended to be social workers or even "Avon Ladies" if the violent man was at home. Other officers described getting a contact address or place and time to meet the victim through the uniformed officers who attended the initial incident.

Twenty-one of the DVOs had an information leaflet for victims with the names and addresses of other agencies who might be able to help them and a brief description of their various legal rights and options. The three officers who did not have leaflets were in the process of producing them.

All of the officers advised victims about their civil law options as well as their criminal law choices, in particular, about obtaining an injunction against their partner. However, most DVOs preferred to put women in touch with solicitors for more detailed and specific advice.

Fifteen of the officers were involved in taking the victim's statement (although most of the officers said they only took retraction statements – given when a victim withdraws or retracts her complaint – rather than the original complaint). Some DVOs said they would take a statement if the woman was particularly frightened or did not want to talk to a uniformed or CID officer. When they did take statements, they all said they would include a history of the violence suffered by the victim.

Most officers (n=19) thought that they should remain neutral and offer advice on the "pros and cons" when the victim was deciding whether to press charges against their partner and whether to give evidence against him – leaving the final decision entirely up to the victim. Various reasons were given for this – centering around empowering the victim and allowing her the right to make her own decisions:

> *"The victim needs a friend at the end of the day and it's not fair to push her or she won't come back."*

Five of the DVOs said they would go as far as to try to encourage the victim to press charges:

> *"...it's better that the court marks his card for him."*

> *"...especially if there is a history of violence but not so much if it is a one-off."*

When it came to the decision about whether to give evidence, half of the officers said that they left the decision entirely to the victim. The other twelve officers said they were willing to encourage the victim to give evidence – feeling that as she had come this far it would be a shame to give up.

Fourteen of the DVOs thought that victims of domestic violence should not be compelled to give evidence, mainly because this would involve taking away her choices. They also thought that a compelled victim would not normally be good for the case. The remaining ten officers thought that in certain circumstances, compelling the victim could be justified, particularly if the case was very serious:

> *"only in the very rare cases .... for example, attempted murder."*

> *"where they're being pressured to retract and there are severe injuries."*

All but one of the officers frequently accompanied victims to court.[1] Officers described their function at court as general support for the victim; explaining the court procedures (often in advance of the trial date); and protecting the victim.

For sixteen of the DVOs, it was force policy to keep the victim informed of the progress of her case. The other officers said that it was not strictly part of their job but that it had simply fallen to them in practice to do. All except one DVO tried to let the victim know about the defendant's bail status, the outcome of any trial, and the sentence received at court.[2] However, because there did not seem to be a system whereby the DVO could automatically obtain this information, only eleven officers said they were able to let the victim know of the release dates of offenders serving custodial sentences.

---

[1] The one officer who could not perform this duty was also a custody sergeant and therefore had to be available at the station when on duty.
[2] The DVO who did not do this said that the investigating officer should keep the victim informed in this way, but that she would be happy to do so if required.

Keeping a record and monitoring arrangements [3]

All the DVOs kept a record of domestic violence incidents in their areas, which included incidents where no further police action had been taken. In two of the forces records were kept manually on a card index, but officers in Northamptonshire had a computer system on which to keep their records. All except one DVO said that these records (both manual and computerised) enabled them to keep a trace on persistent offenders by cross referencing their records by victim, suspect and address.[4] Most of the DVOs also said that uniformed officers sometimes used this information during their investigations.

Most DVOs had to collect domestic violence referral forms or Command and Control prints-out of domestic violence incidents each morning, chase up uniformed officers who had not completed referral forms and then manually record each incident on a card index. This meant that time when DVOs could be seeing and helping victims was being spent recording incidents by hand. In addition, because the DVOs were so reliant on uniformed officers completing forms or Control Room staff recording incidents as domestic violence cases, they were not receiving information about all the domestic violence incidents in their area.

Sometimes domestic violence records were held by DVOs which meant that Command and Control did not always have immediate access to that information when officers were called to attend a domestic violence incident, but instead had to obtain it from the DVO. This also resulted in the situation in one force, whereby DVOs had to physically take their card indexes to the Control Room at night and collect them again the next morning in order that the information could be available out of office hours.

All but two of the DVOs interviewed said that they used their records to monitor the processing of domestic violence cases including rates of arrest, charging and prosecution. This information was only regularly used by the DVOs themselves, many of whom said that their uniformed colleagues did not use the information as much as they should or could.

West Midlands DVOs said that they had to send monthly statistical returns to headquarters and other officers passed the information to their line management – sometimes on request but more often on their own initiative.

Relationship with other officers

The majority of the DVOs (n=17) described their relationship with their uniformed colleagues as "good"; seven described it as "okay" [5]:

> *"...increasingly officers are referring victims to me. I take their workload off them. Police Constables don't have the time to spend enough time with the victims to do the job properly, the domestic violence officer does".*

---

[3] Chapter Three discusses the ways in which police records on domestic violence were kept by each force. This section deals specifically with the ways in which DVOs kept their own records.
[4] The remaining officer did not cross reference her index for offender information.
[5] One officer felt that she had moved to the station too recently to comment.

Many officers said that relationships were improving, although there were still a few "*old dinosaurs*" to deal with and that there was still room for improvement.

Most of the DVOs said that uniformed colleagues came to them for advice on how to deal with domestic violence cases or to update themselves on what had happened with a particular case. Only seven of the DVOs said that they thought uniformed colleagues *always* referred domestic violence cases to them. Eight said that they sometimes did, and nine were sure they were not getting anywhere near all the cases referred to them. Of course, a DVO will only hear about a domestic violence incident if the officers who attended defined it as such.

One DVO's response clearly indicated that she had become very frustrated with the paucity of information reaching her:

> "*No they forget, they are lazy and ignorant. If there is no arrest they do not want to know.*"

Eighteen of the officers were involved in the training of uniformed officers. This training included training probationers at training school or having them spend a day or two working with them; speaking to and updating the uniformed officers on their various shifts; training probationers at training school; and talking to Sergeants and Inspectors to make sure they passed the information to their shifts.

Relationship with the CPS

Nine DVOs described their relationship with the CPS as "good", 12 as "okay", one as "bad" and two as "non-existent". The officer who described it as bad said this was because the CPS had an "obstructive attitude". One officer bypassed the CPS and went straight to court for the information she required and the remaining officer had not yet contacted the CPS for any information but was planning to do so in the future.

Building up a relationship with an individual lawyer who has responsibility for domestic violence cases seemed to be the most fruitful way of developing a good working relationship. However, several officers felt that the CPS did not fully understand the plight of the victim and were overly keen to reduce charges.

Contact and relationships with other agencies

The most frequently contacted agencies were solicitors, housing departments and women's aid/refuges and DVOs were far less reluctant to use women's refuges and/or Women's Aid than their uniformed colleagues (see Table 5.1). DVOs were rarely in contact with Victim Support Schemes or the probation service. Obviously, specialist agencies such as Rape Crisis and counsellors were used less frequently, as fewer victims required their services.

Table 5.1 Frequency of contact with other agencies

	F*	S	R	N
Women's Aid/ Refuges	13	9	2	0
Social Services	7	7	10	0
Victim Support Schemes	7	4	10	3
Solicitors	23	1	0	0
Probation Service	0	5	10	9
GPs/Hospital	7	10	5	2
Rape Crisis Centres	1	6	9	8
Relate	7	8	8	1
Specialist Counsellors**	3	4	8	9
LA Housing	19	5	0	0
Citizen's Advice Bureaux	2	11	8	3
Ethnic Minority Women's Groups	6	4	7	7

Frequently, S=sometimes, R=rarely, N=never

** *specialist counselling = referring women for drugs or alcohol counselling*

Table 5.2 Relationship with other agencies

	Good	Okay	Bad	None*
Women's Aid/ Refuges	21	2	0	1
Social Services	12	7	3	2
Victim Support Schemes	15	7	1	1
Solicitors	20	4	0	0
Probation Service	9	2	0	13
GPs/Hospital	14	5	5	0
Rape Crisis Centres	9	1	2	12
Relate	15	5	0	4
Specialist Counsellors**	8	3	0	13
LA Housing	20	4	0	0
Citizen's Advice Bureaux	12	7	0	5
Ethnic Minority Women's Groups	12	3	0	9

None= respondent did not feel relationship had developed sufficiently to be able to comment due to little or no contact

**specialist counsellors= referring women for drugs or alcohol counselling*

The majority of DVOs were positive about their relationship with Women's Aid/women's refuges despite the past history of tension between Women's Aid and the police. In most cases the more often DVOs were in touch with an agency, the better their relationship seemed to be.

Inter-agency groups

Sixteen DVOs were personally involved in an inter-agency group for domestic violence. All the officers who attended a group found it useful:

> *"yes, very active. All pulling in the same direction. All very interested and genuine. It makes things happen like taking the initiative to work with perpetrators, putting a booklet together, forming the solicitors injunction group."*

With one exception those DVOs who did not belong to a group said that they would like to join one:

"Yes, for feedback from all agencies and to get a better understanding about what they can do and for better liaison."

The one officer who did not want to belong to a group thought that she could do her job perfectly well without it and said that meeting with other agencies "hadn't done me any favours".

Availability and resources

DVOs were available between eight and ten hours per day, usually Monday to Friday but also sometimes on a Saturday. In most cases, two officers were on duty together most of the day (with one coming in earlier and one staying later), but some officers worked alone.

Only nine officers described their facilities as good and seven described them as poor or very poor:

"Reasonable, but there are no facilities for the victim."

"Poor – unfriendly dark room shared with child protection. But never a problem for space and there are plenty of new interview rooms."

Those DVOs who shared facilities with Child Protection Officers often had access to their purpose-built interviewing rooms, victim comfort suites, creche facilities etc. However, these rooms were frequently fully occupied by those carrying out child protection work who seemed to have first call on them. When the DVOs could use them, they felt it did help enormously – as they were private and comfortable and thus helped create a relaxing atmosphere for the victim.

DVOs described various problems which they felt stopped them doing their jobs as well as they would like to do. These problems involved a lack of resources, a lack of staff, the attitude of colleagues, poor facilities and a heavy workload. Many of the officers were not allowed to work paid overtime, although several did extra (unpaid) work. Many DVOs wanted computers to input their records. Having to record incidents manually took up a large amount of time which they felt could be better used talking to victims. Others wanted a more efficient referral system so that they did not have to waste time checking the number of referral forms received and chasing up cases. Some DVOs were located in a separate building to the main station and, while they appreciated that this might encourage victims to come to see them, they also felt that it isolated them from their uniformed colleagues and made contact with them more difficult.

Sixteen of the officers felt that they had enough support from their line managers, three thought that they sometimes did and five thought that they did not. Many of the more experienced officers did not see the need for much day-to-day support and appreciated the fact that their line managers trusted them enough to let them get on with their job without too much interference. When child protection Sergeants who had line management responsibilities for DVOs were interviewed, it was clear that they had little knowledge or interest in the DVOs' work and offered them little support.

Key points

Interviews with DVOs showed them to be strongly committed to their work and keen to support victims in whatever decision they might make. Virtually all of the DVOs interviewed were Constables and therefore had limited authority to tell their uniformed colleagues how they should deal with domestic violence cases. Although the majority of DVOs said that they felt they had the support of their line management, this tended to take the form of leaving most DVOs to "get on with it", which did not help them in their dealing with uniformed officers.

The DVOs interviewed appeared, from observations of their working day, to have a very heavy workload. In particular, those officers who worked alone were struggling to keep up to date with their various tasks. Laborious referral and recording systems made this particularly difficult as our own attempts to extract data emphasised (see Chapter Three).

Most DVOs had attempted to liaise with other agencies in the field [6] and to refer victims on to specialised agencies when necessary. However, it did appear from discussions with the officers that some were taking on too much and were placing too much emphasis on the counselling of the victim – a task for which they had neither the training nor the resources. It also appeared that the DVOs' liaison with other agencies was sometimes better than that with their own colleagues. In many divisions, DVOs seemed isolated and were not always routinely notified of domestic violence incidents in their area. As a result, many women who may need the services of a DVO are not being reached.

Of the three forces examined in this part of the study which had DVOs, only the West Midlands had a DVO in every division. The situations in Northamptonshire and South Yorkshire mean that one woman will be offered the services of a DVO whereas another woman living a few streets away will not.

---

[6] This will be discussed in detail in Chapter Seven, from the viewpoint of the other agencies.

POLICING DOMESTIC VIOLENCE IN THE 1990s

6   The victim's perspective

One of the main themes of Home Office circular 60/1990 was that the police should improve their service to victims of domestic violence. This study included a small survey of the police response viewed by domestic violence victims.

Twenty-three victims of domestic violence were interviewed face-to-face and a further six women completed semi-structured questionnaires.[1] Sixteen women were contacted through the DVOs and 13 through women's refuges. When responses were analysed according to whether the respondents were referred by DVOs or refuges, no clear cut pattern emerged, but the numbers involved mean that the results should be regarded as illustrative rather than representative.

Women were asked about their experiences with the police – both uniformed officers and DVOs; their experiences of the criminal justice system in general; and their contact with other agencies. A brief domestic violence history was also obtained, although interviewers were careful not to cause distress to the respondent by asking very detailed questions about her experiences. Interviews were taped wherever possible and detailed notes were made both during and immediately after the other interviews.

We had hoped to interview victims from ethnic minority groups. However, this proved impossible. None of the DVOs had had contact with women from ethnic minority group – how far this is because such women are reluctant to contact the police is open to question. We did speak to workers at refuges specifically for ethnic minority women. While some of them were willing to ask their clients to talk to us – no women came forward. However, through our discussions with the refuge staff we have been able to obtain some insight into the particular difficulties ethnic minority victims of domestic violence have. Because these discussions are based on the impressions of the *workers* rather than the victims themselves they are included in Chapter Seven.

Background

Most of the 29 women in the sample were young - 16 of them were in their twenties, with half of those under 25 years of age. Five women were in their thirties; one was in her forties and two were in their fifties.[2] Sixteen of the women described themselves as living apart from their partner, with five of these women saying that they had only just separated. A further nine women were divorced or in the process of divorcing their partner; and one woman was hoping to be reconciled with her partner. The marital status of the three remaining respondents was not clear. Only two of the women did not have children.

---

[1] One refuge had a policy of not allowing researchers to speak to their residents as they were concerned that if they did so, the women would be continually bombarded by interviewers. However, they did agree to the women completing a questionnaire and so the checklist used for the face-to-face interviews was adapted to a questionnaire format for the residents to complete.
[2] Age was not available for five of the respondents.

POLICING DOMESTIC VIOLENCE IN THE 1990s

Respondents described relationships with the men who were violent towards them which lasted from less than a year to 33 years. The average length of relationship was nine years. The patterns of violence within those relationships also varied. Nine women described the violence as having occurred throughout the whole length of the relationship and eight women said it had occurred during the latter half of their relationship. Most of the women reported that there had been a period at the beginning of the relationship which had been free from violence. The women often said the violence began at a key stage in their relationship – in particular when they got married or when they were pregnant:

> *"It started when I was pregnant .... I lost a baby twice because of him hitting me."*

Contact with uniformed police

Two of the women had never called the police and had only come into contact with them while staying at a refuge. Seven had only called the police once; nine had called two or three times and six estimated that they had called for help over five times. The remaining five women said that they had lost count of the number of times they had had to call the police.

Many of the women said that they had been very reluctant to call the police, sometimes because they found domestic violence a shaming experience or because they did not want to get their partners into trouble or upset their family. Many of the women also feared the consequences of getting the police involved in the matter.

Of the 21 women who had called the police at some time, most had only called the police in the last year (n=12), but some had been calling them for up to nine years. Equal numbers of women reported good and bad experiences with the police and in fact some had experienced both.

Women who described positive experiences usually felt that the police had taken their situation seriously. For this to happen, it seemed important to the women that the police arrived quickly after they were called:

> *"..and the police came straight away and stayed with me 'til five o'clock in the morning".*

Women who rated their experience of the police as good commented that being listened to – particularly when the police were deciding what action to take – and being offered options in a neutral way without being pressured to make a complaint, was especially important. One woman described being left alone to make her own decisions:

> *"They were absolutely silent because they obviously didn't want to sway me.... the police didn't put words into my mouth at all."*

One woman described how the police had helped her collect her things from her home after she had fled to a refuge. She said that they told her she could press charges if she wished to but she did not feel they had put her under any pressure to do so. They also advised her about her civil law options and said if she needed their help again then she should call on them. This woman felt that her treatment by the police had been ideal in that she had been left to make up her own mind and, despite the fact that she had decided not to press charges, the police had offered continuing support.

A caring attitude from the police was very much appreciated:

"They were absolutely super....they were very gentle the way they interviewed the children ... they were very calming with my husband ... and they were really smashing".

Respondents also appreciated any follow-up from the police after the initial incident. This seemed to encourage them to feel that the police had an on-going interest in their safety.

In contrast, women who related negative experiences of the police talked about a long delay before the police arrived and their unhelpful and dismissive attitude. These women felt that the police appeared reluctant to become involved in a domestic violence incident:

"And I found to be honest that the police's attitude was terrible. It's awful, it's still basically the same as it ever was years ago. Their attitude is still very much that it's a domestic."

Some women said that not only did the police not sympathise with them, but seemed to side with the violent man and make them feel like the criminal. They said that the police often offered their own opinions on who was to blame for the violence. Some women said that they had been threatened with having their children taken away and told that the violence was their own fault:

"When my husband was actually arrested he was interviewed by a young WPC and my husband obviously charmed that young WPC and the young WPC telephoned me after she had spoken to my husband ... she said to me 'in my opinion it is six of one and half a dozen of the other."

Another said:

"Yes, they took me and the children to the police station... and I was made to feel like I was the criminal... you know it was really awful... I was threatened with a hospital and to have my children taken off me... it was really bad."

One woman described an episode where her husband had followed one of their children back to the refuge where they were staying and had refused to go away despite there being an injunction against him with powers of arrest attached. She said that the police were called and that a WPC had arrived and started to talk to her husband outside. The woman said that half an hour later the WPC came into the refuge to tell her that

POLICING DOMESTIC VIOLENCE IN THE 1990s

"her husband really loved her, wanted her back and missed the kids".

Women with bad experiences said that the police were very reluctant to arrest or press charges against the man even if they themselves were eager to do so:

> *"I said I wanted him charged. He [the police officer] said oh I'm not bothering with that. And I said why? And he said to me, because, he said he'll be back kissing your stitches next week."*

Civil and criminal justice processes

Fifteen of the 29 women had had injunctions against their partners at some stage. However, only four of these injunctions had powers of arrest attached to them.[3] The majority of these women said that injunctions were not very useful, often because they felt the police were reluctant to do anything when they were breached:

> *"I explained I'd just obtained an injunction although it wasn't one with powers of arrest attached to it so they [the police] said there wasn't a lot they could do."*

A majority (n=15) of the women whose partners had been arrested at least on one occasion said that they were eager to press charges. However two said that they had lost their nerve and withdrawn their complaint. These arrests and charges resulted in 14 prosecutions and eight convictions.[4] Twelve of the women who supported a prosecution were in touch with a DVO, which suggests that having the support of a DVO may encourage more women to pursue a prosecution.

The most severe penalty received by an offender was a two year custodial sentence for malicious wounding. The least severe sentence, received by two offenders convicted of ABH,[5] was a 12 month conditional discharge plus compensation to the victim. Another offender was bound over for six months. Two women saw their partners found not guilty of assaulting them but guilty of other offences which occurred at the time of the alleged assault. One woman said her partner was found guilty of "violent entry" (and was awaiting sentence) and the other of drunk and disorderly conduct. In the remaining case, the defendant was found guilty of assaulting both his partner and a police officer. He was sentenced to nine months imprisonment for the former offence and 12 months imprisonment (concurrently) for the latter. In addition, one of the women who had dropped the charges against her partner said that she had done so partly because he was charged with assaulting a police officer (for which offence he was sentenced to two years probation) and she felt that the police thought this was far more important than the assault against her:

> *"Yeah, I wasn't important any more - the main focus was all on the police ... the police had come out, something was done against them, and so this had to be carried through".*

---

[3] Without such powers of arrest, there are limits on what the police can do if the violent partner breaks the conditions of the injunction.
[4] Three of the women's partners were awaiting trial at the time of the interview, one defendant was found not guilty and, as already mentioned, two women dropped the charges.
[5] Actual Bodily Harm.

Many of the women commented on how let down they felt by the court process:

> "I was disgusted with what happened to him. He got bound over to keep the peace for six months. I could not understand that, I pressed charges of assault and he got bound over."

> "We went through a trial for six months where he pleaded not guilty and we were constantly going back to court and literally you're made to feel like a criminal, it was awful."

Contact with domestic violence officers

Eighteen of the women had been in contact with a DVO.[6] Eight of the nine women who had not been in contact, lived in force areas which had a DVO. The one woman who was in an area without a DVO said that she would have found it extremely helpful to have had one officer to contact, as every time she called the police she spoke to a different person which she had found very confusing.

The women had found out about the DVOs from various sources – but mainly through the uniformed police officers who had attended the initial incident. Other women were either approached by the DVO or contacted them themselves. The women were all very positive about their contact with DVOs. It was evident from their responses that the DVOs had been helpful, supportive and understanding, even long after the initial event.

> "She's a friend. You know, I haven't seen her for a couple of weeks but I know if I ring her up tomorrow and said I needed to talk, it would be straight away she'd come to me."

Some women admitted that they would never have gone through with a prosecution if they had not had the support of the DVO:

> "Yes, all the times I've been to court Anne [the DVO] has come with me .... I wouldn't have gone if Anne hadn't have been [there]."

One respondent suggested that it would have been very useful for there to have been a woman who had experienced domestic violence available to talk to at the police station after the initial incident had occurred. She felt that this was important as only they could fully understand how a victim felt and could also act as proof that "there was life on the other side". Through one DVO, some women had formed a self-help group and now offered each other advice and support, as well as receiving it from the DVO herself.

A few women did have less positive comments about DVOs. One woman said that she had felt very intimidated by the DVO, who was a "very strong woman". This woman thought that the DVO saw her as weak for not leaving her partner more quickly and viewed male officers as more sympathetic. It should be noted that other victims commented positively on the same DVO's attitude towards them.

---

[6] It should be noted that only two women contacted through a refuge had had contact with a DVO. Also, in two interviews the amount of information about the victim's contact with DVOs is not sufficient to comment on, so these have been excluded from the discussion in this section.

Another woman described how shocked she was when she received a letter from a DVO asking her to come into the station. She had no idea what a DVO was and thought that she might be in trouble with the police herself. Several women made the point that they had not known DVOs existed before they came into contact with the police and thought that their services should be advertised more widely:

"I didn't know that they had a DVO – I mean if I don't know who else doesn't know? Anne should be publicised so that people know she's there."

One respondent said that she felt the DVO role was marginalised by the police and that relying on women to run these units made domestic violence "a woman's problem". She thought that her partner would take far more notice of a male officer than a female:

"I think there should be more male police officers involved in it ... I have spoken to male officers as well that have said more men should be involved in it because it's not just a woman's issue... you get the likes of my husband when the shouting is going on and he just laughs in the face of a woman. But when it's coming from a man and he's saying what you're doing is wrong ... then he'll listen....but he won't listen to a woman."

Contact with women's refuges

The other main agencies with whom the women had contact were women's refuges. Fifteen of the women had had some contact with a refuge.[7] In fact, there appeared to be a natural division between those women who used a refuge as their main source of support and those who used a DVU. It was very rare that a woman had a great deal of contact with both DVUs and refuges, perhaps because their roles overlap (for example as a source of referrals to other agencies).

The women described mixed experiences with various other agencies – housing, social services, victim support and "the welfare people". But their contact with these agencies was on a much more superficial level that with either refuges or the police and it was normally either the DVO or the refuge which put them in touch with these agencies to deal with their specific needs.

Key points

The women's experience of contact with uniformed police appeared to have been very mixed. Although some victims described officers as helpful and non-judgemental and understanding about their needs, others said that they had been dismissive and unsympathetic about what they had been through.

When the police did charge an offender and the case came to court, many respondents felt that the way in which the courts had dealt with their complaints had exacerbated their

---

[7] No distinction was made between those refuges affiliated to Women's Aid and those not as the women often did not know with which type of refuge they had had contact.

problems. It is beyond the scope of this study to discuss this issue in detail, but it is obviously an area of importance and concern.

Most women spoke very positively about their contact with DVOs. It was clear that the women had received a great deal of support and assistance from them. Perhaps one point of concern is that there was little evidence to suggest that DVOs and refuges worked together – but rather that they offered a similar service to victims, who appeared to contact either a refuge or a DVO for help. This could result in a duplication of effort on the parts of the two agencies.

POLICING DOMESTIC VIOLENCE IN THE 1990s

7 How the police are perceived by other agencies

Introduction

One of the recommendations of Home Office circular 60/1990 was that the police should improve their liaison with other agencies dealing with domestic violence. This chapter reports on discussions held with at least one representative from some of those agencies – in particular, the Crown Prosecution Service;[1] women's refuges; local authority housing; and Victim Support Schemes – in each area. As well as these "core" agencies, interviews were also conducted with representatives from agencies who had developed some role in relation to domestic violence in the various force areas. Discussions focused on how the particular agency saw the police's role in respect of domestic violence and their views on how the police actually responded to domestic violence.

Crown Prosecution Service

Views on the police

Each of the five Crown Prosecution Service (CPS) respondents saw themselves and the police in complementary roles – working towards the arrest and prosecution of domestic violence offenders. However, some prosecutors voiced concerns about older police officers being set in their ways. On the other hand they said that younger officers sometimes became quickly disillusioned when victims withdrew their complaints or when they came under the influence of older officers. Prosecutors viewed the police as treating prosecution as the best way to teach the abuser a lesson, but thought it was vital to emphasise to the police that the evidence in domestic violence cases must be of very high quality to ensure the greatest chance of securing a conviction.

Contact with domestic violence officers

Most prosecutors supported the idea of DVOs and had established good working relationships with them. This made liaison and information exchange with the police much easier and prosecutors found the DVOs' detailed knowledge of individual cases very useful. The DVOs often acted as a contact point for the CPS and respondents felt that this ensured a consistency of approach. Most respondents also thought that DVOs aided successful prosecutions by supporting victims throughout the criminal justice process. However, one prosecutor expressed reservations about the role of DVOs and said that he preferred to deal with arresting officers rather than DVOs because they knew more about the initial incident.

---

[1] The CPS were also asked about their own practices because these were so heavily interlinked with those of the police.

POLICING DOMESTIC VIOLENCE IN THE 1990s

Retraction of complaints

All CPS respondents said that they insisted on a formal retraction statement if a victim decided to withdraw her complaint, and would not terminate a case without one. Several admitted that this was a relatively new system and the practice had been rather haphazard in the past. Most also said that they would ask the police to find out the reasons why a victim was withdrawing, to check that she had not been intimidated. Again, DVOs were thought to be best placed to know whether the withdrawal was voluntary. One prosecutor said that she was keen for victims to come to court to withdraw a complaint, as this served to emphasise the seriousness to the victim of making a complaint. However, she had taken account of her local DVO's reservations about this practice and did not insist that it happened.

Most prosecutors said that the best option for victims was to take their violent partners to court and that victims could help to make the system work by not withdrawing their complaints. Prosecutors said that unless the victim co-operated with a prosecution there was very little they could do to help her. However, some prosecutors did say that they felt the CPS could do much more to support victims when they came to court and by doing so they might help to reduce the number of withdrawals.

All the prosecutors said that they would be willing to pursue a case without a victim's support but only if there was independent evidence of an assault (usually a witness) and/or the case was serious enough to warrant going ahead. Most thought that compelling witnesses should be reserved for the most serious cases where the defendant posed a considerable danger to the victim.

Several respondents mentioned that Section 23 of the Criminal Justice Act 1988 allowed written evidence to be offered in court if a witness felt intimidated and did not want to give evidence in person. Some thought that this might be useful in domestic violence cases – but most agreed that judges preferred to see the victim in person and that consequently Section 23 was rarely used.[2]

Charge reduction and bind-overs

All prosecutors said that they were prepared to use the full range of possible offences from, for example, wounding to common assault, in domestic violence cases. However, they explained that the first charge laid would probably be the most serious possible for the given facts, but that this charge might be reduced if a lesser charge "offered appropriate penalties for the injury sustained". In addition, several said that they were very keen to use summary-only offences because it was better to prosecute cases in the magistrates' court where they would be dealt with more speedily and where, one prosecutor said, a conviction was more likely. The same prosecutor described this decision-making process as a balancing act between ensuring a serious enough charge was brought and making sure the case was dealt with swiftly and efficiently – "for the victim's sake".

---

[2] The infrequent use of Section 23 probably also reflects the very strict conditions which need to be fulfilled before it can be applied.

Most prosecutors thought that bind-overs (binding an offender over to keep the peace) could be useful in less serious cases (as this did not require the victim to give evidence) and only one respondent thought that this practice "devalued" the offence. It was generally thought that bind-overs should be considered where the victim was reluctant to give evidence or the evidence was rather weak. However, most prosecutors admitted that a bind-over offered little protection to the victim and would not have any deterrent effect on persistent abusers.

Women's refuges

Background

A variety of refuges were visited. Some were affiliated to Women's Aid and other refuges were "independent" organisations – funded by a charity or by the local authority.

Views on the police

Refuge workers were generally very critical of the police response to domestic violence. However their replies and those of operational police officers (Chapter Four) also showed that there was little direct contact between the police and the refuges.

Respondents said that referrals to refuges were rarely received directly from the police, and many felt that the police did not tell women about the services which they could provide and, moreover, did not have any respect for the work refuges did. Some workers thought that the police only used the refuges in an emergency and did not consider that they could offer anything other than temporary shelter. However, some respondents also said that because they could not allow the police to just "pop round" to the refuge it was difficult to develop good informal relations with the police.

While the refuge workers welcomed the Circular, many felt that the police had only paid lip service to its guidelines; that the police displayed a lack of understanding of domestic violence issues; and were largely ignorant of the law – in particular the civil law; and did not have sufficient training about domestic violence or the recommendations of the Circular. Many said that they were involved in trying to rectify the last of these through offering to train police officers.

Several workers said that most women with whom they came into contact have never called the police - because they did not believe they could help. Most respondents complained that the police were slow to respond to domestic violence calls and cited examples of women waiting up to three hours for the police to arrive.

The workers said that when they did arrive, the police would do nothing without definite evidence of an assault; would not arrest unless there were severe injuries; and were generally not interested unless there was a strong chance of a conviction.

One of the main services the police provided was to act as an escort for refuge clients so that they could collect their belongings (and sometimes their children) from home. While some respondents said that the police carried out this function very well and were quick to respond to such requests, others said that they were always reluctant to do it, and often sided with the violent partner when they took the woman to her house. Several respondents thought that the police were keener to help if there were children involved and said that women with children were generally more satisfied with the response they had from the police. This corresponds with the responses from operational officers who saw the joint safety of the woman and her children as their main priority.

Several respondents said that the police were very good at offering advice to both individual women and the refuges about security and at dealing with cases where the injuries were severe and prosecution was very likely. However, they said that because domestic violence was not like other crimes (which tend to be one-off events) the police found dealing with them very difficult.

One respondent made an observation about the kinds of cases in which the police were usually involved which she felt might go some way to explaining why they find dealing with such cases so difficult. She said that often, the women the police refer to the refuge are in a state of immediate crisis - leaving home without preparation or forethought. Women in this position, the worker considered, are most likely to return to their partners, unlike those who come directly to the refuges having planned their escape over a period of time. The respondent felt that because the police come into contact most frequently with women in crisis they see a lot of women returning home and they therefore become cynical about what can be done to help them and are then less keen to get involved in other cases.

Contact with DVOs

The refuge workers' rated their contact with DVOs more positively than their contact with general officers and many had developed good working relationships with a DVO. Because of this, they had become less reluctant to work with the police in general. Most of the referrals which came from the police came via DVOs. However, several workers felt that DVOs were often marginalised from and unsupported by the rest of the police and therefore had little impact on the general police response.

Asian women's refuges

In the main, the problems described by workers in refuges for Asian women were similar to those for general refuges but were thought to be further exacerbated by the particular sensitivities associated with domestic violence in Asian communities. Workers said that the police failed to appreciate sensitivities about violence in Asian families. Ironically, this meant that the police were sometimes more helpful to women trying to leave such families, as they thought this was their best option. On the other hand, respondents said that the police sometimes seemed very reluctant to get involved, knowing that any action they took could have repercussions for their dealings with the Asian community as a whole.

One worker said that it was very important for the address of the refuge to be kept secret because if it became known in the wider Asian community it would soon become known to the violent partner. She said that the police had often given the address to inappropriate people.

Local authority housing departments

Background

Most housing departments deal with domestic violence victims through their homelessness units. Women fleeing violence are no longer regarded as "intentionally homeless" (which used to be a general housing policy).

Views on the police

Most housing workers said that very few of the domestic violence victims they saw spoke highly of the police and that the perception that the police will do little to help was still very prevalent. However, most also said that they thought the police response was improving but that policy changes had been slow to reach the lower ranks in the police and that a cultural and attitudinal change was still required among these officers. The number of referrals they received from the police had increased, particularly in areas with DVOs, with whom several officers were in regular contact. The police also seemed more prepared to escort victims to their homes.

Respondents said that DVOs were particularly helpful in verifying victims' stories and had speeded up and simplified this procedure greatly. Many said that they often referred their clients to DVOs for further advice and also received clients via the DVOs. Several workers mentioned having liaised with DVOs about fitting panic alarms in victims' houses.

Victim Support Schemes

Background

All of the Victim Support (VS) workers interviewed described themselves as being at the very early stages of developing a response to domestic violence victims. This corresponds with the DVO's comments about having very little to do with VS in respect of domestic violence.

VS workers in all five areas described a similar arrangement with the police in that each morning they receive a print out of the previous day's incidents. Some forces now "flag up" domestic violence cases and the police seem generally more keen for VS to get involved with domestic violence victims than previously – although in some areas it was thought that the police were still reluctant to pass such cases on to VS.

Most VS schemes will not contact a victim unless she has given her consent to the police to pass on her details to VS. VS then write to the victim and arrange a meeting – usually on neutral ground (i.e. not at a police station or the victim's home). One point to note is that most schemes do not allow their volunteers to contact victims of domestic violence if the perpetrator is still at large. This severely restricts the amount of work they can do with domestic violence victims. Several workers felt that they would have to change this policy as referrals increased.

Views on the police

Overall, VS described an improving police response to domestic violence. However, some thought that the police were not properly trained to deal with domestic violence and that many officers were still unaware of the complexities of the domestic violence situations.

Contact with DVOs was mixed. Some workers said they had established a good system whereby the two agencies worked well together and ensured that there was little duplication of effort. Most thought that having a DVO as a contact point within the police was very useful and ensured a better flow of information between the agencies. However, in some areas respondents said there was very little contact between VS and the DVOs and it appeared that no thought had been put to the possibility that there was an overlap in the work they did. In addition, one worker felt that DVOs took on a VS role when dealing with domestic violence cases and that this was inappropriate. This worker also thought that DVOs pushed victims too hard to support a prosecution instead of offering neutral advice.

Other agencies

As well interviewing representatives from the "core" agencies in each area, contact was also made with particular agencies which had developed some role in domestic violence issues in some of the force areas.

Social services refuge liaison officer

One area had appointed a refuge liaison officer within their social services community support team, whose job it was to work with refuges and other voluntary agencies to help them improve their services for domestic violence victims.[3]

The liaison officer thought that the police were not sufficiently accountable for their dealings with domestic violence cases and that they continued to apply their discretion in the way they did before Circular 60/1990 was issued. She was actively involved in training both existing police officers and new recruits about how to deal with domestic violence incidents. She thought that this was beginning to have an effect and that assumptions and stereotypes held by the police were being effectively challenged.

Women's advice centres

Workers in two Advice Centres were interviewed. The first was funded by Safer Cities to work as a domestic violence counsellor within a general women's advice centre –

---

[3] Consideration was initially given to interviewing social services representatives in all areas. However, a first meeting with a social services representative showed that social services had little to do with domestic violence cases unless that violence forms part of a general family problem or a child abuse case.

offering advice over the phone; running groups for and with domestic violence survivors; and acting as an information resource for women experiencing domestic violence. The other advice centre was run by Women's Aid and offers a crisis intervention facility as well as general advice.

The police had initially contacted the counsellor at the "general" centre and she now refers women on to the DVOs where appropriate. While she was very positive about her contact with DVOs she felt that the police in general could not deal with domestic violence effectively.

The Women's Aid worker said that while the police were now more open and responsive to other agencies asking for help in domestic violence cases, she was less certain that they helped women who did not have the support of these other agencies. In particular, she felt that the police were most reluctant to deal with women who did not conform to a passive victim's role. This worker was also concerned about the inaccuracy of some of the advice the police give to victims. She said the centre had offered to help with training but so far their offer had not been taken up. She also saw a clash between victims' needs and the police agenda – the victims want protection and the police want prosecutions.

Safer Cities

In one area, Safer Cities had identified women's safety as one of their priorities and thus became involved in work on domestic violence. This involvement mainly comprised setting up a support group for workers in the field from various agencies and funding two surveys looking at women's experiences of domestic violence. The co-ordinator's main criticism of the police was that they went about their work unilaterally and gave the impression that they were the experts and had nothing to learn from other agencies. For example, she said that they had refused the offer of joint training saying that it was not needed. She also made the point that there was a danger of spending too much time worrying about the police's role vis-à-vis domestic violence since their role is in most cases very limited.

Solicitors' injunction group

Solicitors in one area have formed a group which is committed to dealing with domestic violence victims within 24 hours of them calling, or finding another solicitor to do so if they cannot. The organiser of the group said that the police had come to them for information and advice on the use of injunctions and that she had been involved in training the police about how to use the civil law effectively in domestic violence cases. She felt that it was important to encourage them to appreciate that failure to deploy the criminal law does not amount to failure to deal with the particular case. At present, she feels that the police are insufficiently informed about injunctions and often think that if an injunction does not carry powers of arrest then there is nothing they can do.

POLICING DOMESTIC VIOLENCE IN THE 1990s

Inter-agency working and inter-agency groups

Most respondents said that the police showed a marked reluctance to be involved in inter-agency working and many felt that they did not have a serious commitment to this kind of work. However, in some areas – particularly those with DVOs – the police were now involved. Indeed, it was sometimes the police who had initiated contact with other agencies.

Many respondents spoke positively about inter-agency groups. Bringing the different agencies together was thought to provide a useful forum for information exchange and participants were able to learn more about what other agencies could do and how their role fitted in with their own. Such meetings were helpful in raising awareness about domestic violence and regular meetings helped to keep domestic violence at the top of everyone's agenda. It was thought that inter-agency groups could improve the working relationships between organisations, develop mutual understanding and a common way of dealing with domestic violence. In particular, by developing joint training, a consistent approach could be developed. By pooling resources, agencies were able to develop initiatives together which they could not do on their own.

Key points

From the findings reported here, it appears that there is further scope for the development of good relationships between the police and other agencies and in ensuring that other agencies believe the police are dealing with domestic violence incidents properly and effectively. While most respondents accepted that the police had developed good policies on domestic violence, they were less convinced that these had been translated into practice. Relations seemed particularly poor with workers in women's refuges. There seemed to be little contact and little mutual understanding.

It was widely thought that DVOs had improved liaison with the police in most areas, and respondents were generally far more satisfied with the response they received from these officers. However, many commented on what little impact the DVOs appeared to have on the general police response.

The CPS appeared to be generally satisfied with both the police's and their own response to domestic violence cases. However, some said that they could improve their performance by actively supporting victims through the criminal justice process. While insisting that they were prepared to use the full array of charges against defendants in domestic violence cases, most felt that it was better for everyone involved if cases were dealt with in the magistrates' court. By default, this meant they favoured using summary-only offences.

Most respondents saw police involvement in inter-agency work as having obvious benefits – improving understanding between agencies and developing a more consistent approach for dealing with domestic violence.

8 Conclusions and implications for good practice

This chapter draws together conclusions from the research and offer examples of current good practice. Some suggestions for future good practice are also given.

The general police response

Virtually all forces have developed policies on domestic violence which closely adhere to the recommendations in Home Office Circular 60/1990. However, the findings in this report suggest that the translation of this policy into practice has been limited. Just over half of the forces had a specialist unit with *some* responsibility for domestic violence but only five forces had domestic violence units dedicated solely to this offence. While there was a general awareness among officers about how domestic violence *should* be policed, this awareness was not always reflected in the way they dealt with such cases. It appeared that managers were overly optimistic about how effective they had been in getting the message across to their operational colleagues and were somewhat out of touch about what was happening at ground level.

Most officers felt that the policing of domestic violence had improved and that such incidents were now being taken more seriously with more positive intervention and more support and advice available for victims. There was evidence that officers had increased their awareness of domestic violence issues and showed a greater understanding and sympathy for victims. However, a third of operational officers had not heard of Circular 60/1990 at all and over half said that they had not received any new guidelines on domestic violence - despite their managers' confidence that the guidance had been successfully disseminated.

Communication between the "policy" and the "practice" ranks could be further developed. Instead of simply introducing a new policy when it is first issued, regular "refresher" sessions need to be implemented. Alongside this, more attention needs to be given to training. As the interviews in Chapter Four show, very few generalist officers have received specific training on domestic violence. Yet many of the other agencies interviewed were willing and able to help with such training. Taking up some of these offers might not only benefit the police's approach to domestic violence but might also help to foster a better understanding between them and other agencies.

Current recording practices make it difficult to know the extent to which domestic violence incidents are reported to the police and result in an arrest, charge or conviction. Increasing the efficiency with which domestic violence cases are recorded and monitored could make it easier to check whether cases were being dealt with properly by, for example, giving a monthly arrest rate or charge rate. Improved recording practices would also enable officers to find out about previous incidents before they attend a domestic violence case. In the current study only a quarter of operational officers said that they were consistently able to check police records for any previous history of assaults <u>before</u> attending a domestic violence incident. Knowing the "historical context" of cases in this way ensures that officers are aware of the seriousness and long term nature of domestic violence situations.

Of the five forces, Northamptonshire has the most sophisticated system of recording. When officers attend domestic violence incidents they are meant to complete a proforma (a "dom1" form) which details various factors of the incident. The proforma is then passed to the DVO who inputs the information onto a computer. This information is then updated as the case progresses through the criminal justice system or as further incidents occur. It can also be used for checking previous incidents when officers attend domestic violence cases. However, even this system could be improved in two ways. First, the DVO's computer could be linked to the main Command and Control system which records all calls for assistance made to the police. In this way, the control room staff could more readily check for past incidents when a call comes through and pass on any relevant information to the officer attending the scene. Second, a completely separate classification of domestic violence could be used in the Command and Control system. Most systems presently "lose" the more serious domestic violence cases as they are re-classified under the various assault categories. It would be then relatively simply to check whether "dom1" forms were being completed for all incidents attended, by comparing them with the incident log from the Command and Control system.[1]

Although most officers were aware that arrest should be a priority in domestic violence cases, almost half of them put it below all other considerations (e.g. the safety of the victim and any children) when asked to prioritise their actions at a domestic violence scene. Their decision to arrest appeared to be heavily influenced by whether a complainant would support any police action. However, the use of informal responses to domestic violence incidents appeared from interviews to be unsatisfactory both for officers – who will usually have to return to that address at a later date – and for victims – who feel the police have not taken their plight seriously enough. If they are to follow the guidance in Circular 60/1990, officers need to consider arrest more often in domestic violence cases. In addition, it may be worth placing less emphasis on Breach of the Peace as a solution and making more use of assault charges. This will reassure the victim that her situation is being taken seriously, and may also have more of a long term impact on her assailant. CPS lawyers did say that, while Breach of the Peace was a speedy way of dealing with domestic violence cases, it probably did not help the victim in the long term nor was it likely to act as a deterrent.

The role of the domestic violence officer

The DVOs interviewed were extremely committed to their work and offered a great deal of long-term support to the victims with whom they came into contact - including taking

---

[1] An alternative model developed by Merseyside police using a separate domestic violence database is described in Lloyd *et al* (1994).

them to court; advising them about their civil and criminal rights; and referring them on to specialist agencies. Interviews with victims, the police and other agencies all indicated that DVOs have become a very important part of an effective police response to domestic violence. However, those DVOs who worked within FPUs, whilst benefiting from the facilities available to them often felt that their work had a lower priority than child protection work, with FPU Sergeants showing little interest or understanding of the work of their DVO subordinates.

The findings reported here suggest that, as yet, DVOs have had little impact on the general police response to domestic violence. One way of increasing their impact is for DVOs to ensure that they keep uniformed colleagues informed of the progress of cases in which they have been involved, show them that successful outcomes are possible and informing them about the work a DVO does. To facilitate this, it is important to locate DVUs in the main station rather than in separate buildings (as has been done in some forces). Finally, rather than relying purely on an individual DVO's ability to "network", it would seem sensible to have a structured, clearly defined system of information exchange and feedback between uniformed and specialist officers throughout all ranks.

Another option may be to follow the example set by the West Midlands force which operates a system of attachments, whereby officers from the uniformed branches come to the DVU for a period of between three to six months to work alongside DVOs. This seems to be very successful in making generalist officers understand and appreciate what DVOs do - a message which they can then take back to their uniformed shift and also use to improve their own response.

The majority of DVOs appeared to be "victims of their own success". Those working alone found it very difficult to cope with the volume of work they had. Ideally, two DVOs should work together. Not only does this lighten the burden, but it also ensures that one officer is available most of the time (if the other officer is on leave or off sick). It also means that the DVU can be open longer hours – as the officers can work shifts and over weekends.

DVOs could help themselves by not taking on every aspect of the victim's care and referring her on to other agencies who may be better qualified to help her. For example, many DVOs talked about needing training in counselling skills. To some extent this is sensible in that a DVO needs to know how to speak to a woman who may be very traumatised, but it may be better for DVOs to refer victims to other agencies who are better qualified to offer any indepth counselling the victim may need or want.

Finally, it is difficult to justify having a service for domestic violence victims in one division and not in another. It may be sensible therefore for Chief Officers to appoint DVOs in *each* of their divisions - as they have in the West Midlands - rather than leave the decision to the discretion of the area commander. Some flexibility in the tenure of DVO posts may also be useful, so that officers themselves could decide when they wanted to move on within say, a five year maximum period.

POLICING DOMESTIC VIOLENCE IN THE 1990s

What do victims want?

The clearest message to emerge from interviews with victims was that they wanted the police to treat their situations seriously and to take into account their needs and wishes when deciding what action to take. An understanding, sympathetic attitude from the police seems to help ensure that victims feel satisfied with the response they receive. The police should be able to offer long-term support to victims – regardless of whether victims decide to pursue a criminal solution to their problems. To offer this support, officers need to know about the various non-criminal options available to victims and support them in whatever decision they decide to take. Nottinghamshire police have established a 24 hour follow-up visit to domestic violence victims which may help to demonstrate an on-going concern for the victim's welfare.

Finally, the availability of DVOs appears, above all other factors, to ensure that victims are more satisfied with their treatment at the hands of the police.

Working with other agencies

Working together can improve the response of all agencies in the field of domestic violence, including the police. One of the best ways in which to actively co-operate with other agencies appears to be through joint training. This is perhaps the best way to develop a common approach and understanding about domestic violence issues. In addition, inter-agency groups can work well in developing, for example, joint initiatives. Both the Nottinghamshire and South Yorkshire forces have been particularly active in their inter-agency domestic violence groups and thus have improved relations between the police and other agencies. South Yorkshire have also attempted to reach both practitioners and policy makers through their groups by having individuals groups in each of the force's divisions each of which feeds into a large group for the whole force area.

It is important to bear in mind when developing inter-agency work that very few victims of domestic violence actually go to the police directly and therefore all agencies need to be able to respond as effectively as possible to calls for help. Alongside this is the fact that the police offer the only 24 hour service for victims of domestic violence and so by improving their response they may be able to help prevent some of the hundred or so female domestic homicides each year.

References

Barclay, G.C. (ed) (1993) Digest 2: *information on the criminal justice system in England and Wales.* Home Office Research and Statistics Department. London:HMSO.

Dobash. R.E. and Dobash, R (1992) *Women, Violence and Social Change.* London: Routledge.

Edwards, S.S.M. (1986) *The Police Response to Domestic Violence in London.* London: Central London Polytechnic.

Edwards, S.S.M. (1989) *Policing 'Domestic' Violence: women, the law and the state.* London: Sage.

Hamner, J. Radford, J. and Stanko, E.A. (1989) *Women, Policing and Male Violence: international perspectives.* London:Routledge.

Home Affairs Committee (1993) *Domestic Violence Vol 1: Report together with the proceedings of the committee.* London: HMSO.

Mayhew, P.; Aye Maung, N. and Mirrlees-Black, C. (1993) *The 1992 British Crime Survey.* Home Office Research Study No. 132. London:HMSO

Mirrlees-Black, C. (1994) 'Estimating the Extent of Domestic Violence: findings from the 1992 BCS.' *Home Office Research Bulletin* No.37. London: Home Office Research and Statistics Department.

Morley, R. and Mullender, A. (1994) *Preventing Domestic Violence to Women.* Police Research Group Crime Prevention Series: Paper No.48. London:HMSO.

Sheptycki, J. (1993) *Innovations in Policing Domestic Violence: evidence from metropolitan London.* Aldershot: Avebury.

Smith, L. (1989) *Domestic Violence.* Home Office Research Study No.107. London: HMSO.

Southgate, P. (1986) *Police – public encounters.* Home Office Research Study No. 77. London: HMSO.

Publications

The Research and Planning Unit (previously the Research Unit) has been publishing its work since 1955, and a full list of Papers is provided below. These reports are available on request from the Home Office Research and Planning Unit, Information Section, Room 278, 50 Queen Anne's Gate, London SW1H 9AT. Telephone: 0171-273 2084 (answerphone).

Reports published in the HORS series are available from HMSO, who will advise as to prices, at the following address: :

HMSO Publications Centre
PO Box 276
London SW8 5DT

Telephone orders: 071-873 9090

General enquiries: 071-873 0011

Titles already published for the Home Office

Studies in the Causes of Delinquency and the Treatment of Offenders (SCDTO)

1. Prediction methods in relation to borstal training. Hermann Mannheim and Leslie T. Wilkins. 1955. viii + 276pp. (11 340051 9).

2. Time spent awaiting trial. Evelyn Gibson. 1960. v + 45pp. (34-368-2).

3. Delinquent generations. Leslie T. Wilkins. 1960. iv + 20pp. (11 340053 5).

4. Murder. Evelyn Gibson and S. Klein. 1961. iv + 44pp. (11 340054 3).

5. Persistent criminals. A study of all offenders liable to preventive detention in 1956. W.H. Hammond and Edna Chayen. 1963. ix + 237pp. (34-368-5).

6. Some statistical and other numerical techniques for classifying individuals. P. McNaughton-Smith. 1965. v + 33pp (34-368-6).

7. Probation research: a preliminary report. Part I. General outline of research. Part II. Study of Middlesex probation area (SOMPA). Steven Folkard, Kate Lyon, Margaret M. Carver and Erica O'Leary. 1966. vi + 58pp. (11 340374 7).

8. Probation research: national study of probation. Trends and regional comparisons in probation (England and Wales). Hugh Barr and Erica O'Leary. 1966. vii + 51pp. (34-368-8).

9. Probation research. A survey of group work in the probation service. Hugh Barr. 1966. vii + 94pp. (34-368-9).

10. Types of delinquency and home background. A validation study of Hewitt and Jenkins' hypothesis. Elizabeth Field. 1967. vi + 21pp. (34-368-10).

11. Studies of female offenders. No. 1 - Girls of 16-20 years sentenced to borstal or detention centre training in 1963. No. 2 - Women offenders in the Metropolitan Police District in March and April 1957. No. 3 - A description of women in prison on January 1, 1965. Nancy Goodman and Jean Price. 1967. v + 78pp. (34-368-11).

12. The use of the Jesness Inventory on a sample of British probationers. Martin Davies. 1967. iv + 20pp. (34-368-12).

13. The Jesness Inventory: application to approved school boys. Joy Mott. 1969. iv + 27pp. (11 340063 2).

Home Office Research Studies (HORS)

(Nos 1–106 are out of print)

1. Workloads in children's departments. Eleanor Grey. 1969. vi + 75pp. (11 340101 9).

2. Probationers in their social environment. A study of male probationers aged 17-20, together with an analysis of those reconvicted within twelve months. Martin Davies. 1969. vii + 204pp. (11 340102 7).

3. Murder 1957 to 1968. A Home Office Statistical Division report on murder in England and Wales. Evelyn Gibson and S. Klein (with annex by the Scottish Home and Health Department on murder in Scotland). 1969. vi + 94pp. (11 340103 5).

4. Firearms in crime. A Home Office Statistical Division report on indictable offences involving firearms in England and Wales. A. D. Weatherhead and B. M. Robinson. 1970. viii + 39pp. (11 340104 3).

5. Financial penalties and probation. Martin Davies. 1970. vii + 39pp. (11 340105 1).

6. Hostels for probationers. A study of the aims, working and variations in effectiveness of male probation hostels with special reference to the influence of the environment on delinquency. Ian Sinclair. 1971. x + 200pp. (11 340106 X).

7. Prediction methods in criminology – including a prediction study of young men on probation. Frances H. Simon. 1971. xi + 234pp. (11 340107 8).

8. Study of the juvenile liaison scheme in West Ham 1961-65. Marilyn Taylor. 1971. vi + 46pp. (11 340108 6).

9. Explorations in after-care. I - After-care units in London, Liverpool and Manchester. Martin Silberman (Royal London Prisoners' Aid Society) and Brenda Chapman.

II - After-care hostels receiving a Home Office grant. Ian Sinclair and David Snow (HORU). III - St. Martin of Tours House, Aryeh Leissner (National Bureau for Co-operation in Child Care). 1971. xi + 140pp. (11 340109 4).

10. A survey of adoption in Great Britain. Eleanor Grey in collaboration with Ronald M. Blunden. 1971. ix + 168pp. (11 340110 8).

11. Thirteen-year-old approved school boys in 1960s. Elizabeth Field, W. H. Hammond and J. Tizard. 1971. ix + 46pp. (11 340111 6).

12. Absconding from approved schools. R. V. G. Clarke and D. N. Martin. 1971. vi + 146pp. (11 340112 4).

13. An experiment in personality assessment of young men remanded in custody. H. Sylvia Anthony. 1972. viii + 79pp. (11 340113 2).

14. Girl offenders aged 17-20 years. I - Statistics relating to girl offenders aged 17-20 years from 1960 to 1970. II - Re-offending by girls released from borstal or detention centre training. III - The problems of girls released from borstal training during their period on after-care. Jean Davies and Nancy Goodman. 1972. v + 77pp. (11 340114 0).

15. The controlled trial in institutional research - paradigm or pitfall for penal evaluators? R. V. G. Clarke and D. B. Cornish. 1972. v + 33pp. (11 340115 9).

16. A survey of fine enforcement. Paul Softley. 1973. v + 65pp. (11 340116 7).

17. An index of social environment - designed for use in social work research. Martin Davies. 1973. vi + 63pp. (11 340117 5).

18. Social enquiry reports and the probation service. Martin Davies and Andrea Knopf. 1973. v + 49pp. (11 340118 3).

19. Depression, psychopathic personality and attempted suicide in a borstal sample. H. Sylvia Anthony.1973. viii + 44pp. (0 11 340119 1).

20. The use of bail and custody by London magistrates' courts before and after the Criminal Justice Act 1967. Frances Simon and Mollie Weatheritt. 1974. vi + 78pp. (0 11 340120 5).

21. Social work in the environment.A study of one aspect of probation practice. Martin Davies, with Margaret Rayfield, Alaster Calder and Tony Fowles. 1974. ix + 151pp. (0 11 340121 3).

22. Social work in prison. An experiment in the use of extended contact with offenders. Margaret Shaw.1974. viii + 154pp. (0 11 340122 1).

23. Delinquency amongst opiate users. Joy Mott and Marilyn Taylor. 1974.vi + 31pp. (0 11 340663 0).

24. IMPACT. Intensive matched probation and after-care treatment. Vol. I - The design of the probation experiment and an interim evaluation. M. S. Folkard, A. J. Fowles, B.C. McWilliams, W. McWilliams, D. D. Smith, D. E. Smith and G. R. Walmsley. 1974. v + 54pp. (0 11 340664 9).

25. The approved school experience. An account of boys' experiences of training under differing regimes of approved schools,with an attempt to evaluate the effectiveness of that training. Anne B. Dunlop. 1974. vii + l24pp. (0 11 340665 7).

26. Absconding from open prisons. Charlotte Banks, Patricia Mayhew and R. J. Sapsford. 1975. viii + 89pp. (0 11 340666 5).

27. Driving while disqualified. Sue Kriefman. 1975. vi + 136pp. (0 11 340667 3).

28. Some male offenders' problems. – Homeless offenders in Liverpool. W. McWilliams. II - Casework with short-term prisoners. Julie Holborn. 1975. x + 147pp. (0 11 340668 1).

29. Community service orders. K. Pease, P. Durkin, I. Earnshaw, D. Payne and J. Thorpe. 1975. viii + 80pp. (0 11 340669 X).

30. Field Wing Bail Hostel: the first nine months. Frances Simon and Sheena Wilson. 1975. viii + 55pp. (0 11 340670 3).

31. Homicide in England and Wales 1967-1971. Evelyn Gibson. 1975. iv + 59pp. (0 11 340753 X).

32. Residential treatment and its effects on delinquency. D. B. Cornish and R. V. G. Clarke. 1975. vi + 74pp. (0 11 340672 X).

33. Further studies of female offenders. Part A: Borstal girls eight years after release. Nancy Goodman, Elizabeth Maloney and Jean Davies. Part B: The sentencing of women at the London Higher Courts. Nancy Goodman, Paul Durkin and Janet Halton. Part C: Girls appearing before a juvenile court. Jean Davies. 1976. vi + 114pp. (0 11 340673 8).

34. Crime as opportunity. P. Mayhew, R. V. G. Clarke, A. Sturman and J. M. Hough. 1976. vii + 36pp. (0 11 340674 6).

35. The effectiveness of sentencing: a review of the literature. S. R. Brody. 1976. v + 89pp. (0 1 340675 4).

36. IMPACT. Intensive matched probation and after-care treatment. Vol. II - The results of the experiment. M. S. Folkard, D. E. Smith and D. D. Smith 1976. xi + 40pp. (0 11 340676 2).

37. Police cautioning in England and Wales. J. A. Ditchfield. 1976. v + 31pp. (0 11 340677 0).

38. Parole in England and Wales. C. P. Nuttall, with E. E. Barnard, A. J. Fowles,

A. Frost, W. H. Hammond, P. Mayhew, K. Pease, R. Tarling and M. J. Weatheritt. 1977. vi + 90pp. (0 11 340678 9).

39. Community service assessed in 1976. K. Pease, S. Billingham and I. Earnshaw. 1977. vi + 29pp. (0 11 340679 7).

40. Screen violence and film censorship: a review of research. Stephen Brody. 1977. vii + 179pp. (0 11 340680 0).

41. Absconding from borstals. Gloria K. Laycock. 1977. v + 82pp. (0 11 340681 9).

42. Gambling: a review of the literature and its implications for policy and research. D. B. Cornish. 1978. xii + 284pp. (0 11 340682 7).

43. Compensation orders in magistrates' courts. Paul Softley. 1978. v + 41pp. (0 11 340683 5).

44. Research in criminal justice. John Croft. 1978. iv + 16pp. (0 11 340684 3).

45. Prison welfare: an account of an experiment at Liverpool. A. J. Fowles. 1978. v + 34pp. (0 11 340685 1).

46. Fines in magistrates' courts. Paul Softley. 1978. v + 42pp. (0 11 340686 X).

47. Tackling vandalism. R. V. Clarke (editor), F. J. Gladstone, A. Sturman and Sheena Wilson 1978. vi + 91pp. (0 11 340687 8).

48. Social inquiry reports: a survey. Jennifer Thorpe. 1979. vi + 55pp. (0 11 340688 6).

49. Crime in public view. P. Mayhew, R. V. G. Clarke, J. N. Burrows, J. M. Hough and S. W. C. Winchester. 1979. v + 36pp. (0 11 340689 4).

50. Crime and the community. John Croft. 1979. v + 16pp. (0 11 340690 8).

51. Life-sentence prisoners. David Smith (editor), Christopher Brown, Joan Worth, Roger Sapsford and Charlotte Banks (contributors). 1979. iv + 51pp. (0 11 340691 6).

52. Hostels for offenders. Jane E. Andrews, with an appendix by Bill Sheppard. 1979. v + 30pp. (0 11 340692 4).

53. Previous convictions, sentence and reconviction: a statistical study of a sample of 5,000 offenders convicted in January 1971. G. J. O. Phillpotts and L. B. Lancucki. 1979. v + 55pp. (0 11 340693 2).

54. Sexual offences, consent and sentencing. Roy Walmsley and Karen White. 1979. vi + 77pp. (0 11 340694 0).

55. Crime prevention and the police. John Burrows, Paul Ekblom and Kevin Heal. 1979. v + 37pp. (0 11 340695 9).

56. Sentencing practice in magistrates' courts. Roger Tarling, with the assistance of Mollie Weatheritt. 1979. vii + 54pp. (0 11 340696 7).

57. Crime and comparative research. John Croft. 1979. iv + 16pp. (0 11 340697 5).

58. Race, crime and arrests. Philip Stevens and Carole F. Willis. 1979. v + 69pp. (0 11 340698 3).

59. Research and criminal policy. John Croft. 1980. iv + 14pp. (0 11 340699 1).

60. Junior attendance centres. Anne B. Dunlop. 1980. v + 47pp. (0 11 340700 9).

61. Police interrogation: an observational study in four police stations. Paul Softley, with the assistance of David Brown, Bob Forde, George Mair and David Moxon. 1980. vii + 67pp. (0 11 340701 7).

62. Co-ordinating crime prevention efforts. F. J. Gladstone. 1980. v + 74pp. (0 11 340702 5).

63. Crime prevention publicity: an assessment. D. Riley and P. Mayhew. 1980. v + 47pp. (0 11 340703 3).

64. Taking offenders out of circulation. Stephen Brody and Roger Tarling. 1980. v + 46pp. (0 11 340704 1).

65. Alcoholism and social policy: are we on the right lines? Mary Tuck. 1980. v + 30pp. (0 11 340705 X).

66. Persistent petty offenders. Suzan Fairhead. 1981. vi + 78pp. (0 11 340706 8).

67. Crime control and the police. Pauline Morris and Kevin Heal. 1981. v + 71pp. (0 11 340707 6).

68. Ethnic minorities in Britain: a study of trends in their position since 1961. Simon Field, George Mair, Tom Rees and Philip Stevens. 1981. v + 48pp. (0 11 340708 4).

69. Managing criminological research. John Croft. 1981. iv + 17pp. (0 11 340709 2).

70. Ethnic minorities, crime and policing: a survey of the experiences of West Indians and whites. Mary Tuck and Peter Southgate. 1981. iv + 54pp. (0 11 340765 3).

71. Contested trials in magistrates' courts. Julie Vennard. 1982. v + 32pp. (0 11 340766 1).

72 Public disorder: a review of research and a study in one inner city area. Simon Field and Peter Southgate. 1982. v + 77pp. (0 11 340767 X).

73. Clearing up crime. John Burrows and Roger Tarling. 1982. vii + 31pp. (0 11 340768 8).

74. Residential burglary: the limits of prevention. Stuart Winchester and Hilary Jackson. 1982. v + 47pp. (0 11 340769 6).

75. Concerning crime. John Croft. 1982. iv + 16pp. (0 11 340770 X).

76. The British Crime Survey: first report. Mike Hough and Pat Mayhew. 1983. v + 62pp. (0 11 340786 6).

77. Contacts between police and public: findings from the British Crime Survey. Peter Southgate and Paul Ekblom. 1984. v + 42pp. (0 11 340771 8).

78. Fear of crime in England and Wales. Michael Maxfield. 1984. v + 57pp. (0 11 340772 6).

79. Crime and police effectiveness. Ronald V. Clarke and Mike Hough 1984. iv + 33pp. (0 11 340773 3).

80. The attitudes of ethnic minorities. Simon Field. 1984. v + 49pp. (0 11 340774 2).

81. Victims of crime: the dimensions of risk. Michael Gottfredson. 1984. v + 54pp. (0 11 340775 0).

82. The tape recording of police interviews with suspects: an interim report. Carole Willis.1984. v + 45pp. (0 11 340776 9).

83. Parental supervision and juvenile delinquency. David Riley and Margaret Shaw. 1985. v + 90pp. (0 11 340799 8).

84. Adult prisons and prisoners in England and Wales 1970-1982: a review of the findings of social research. Joy Mott. 1985. vi + 73pp. (0 11 340801 3).

85. Taking account of crime: key findings from the 1984 British Crime Survey. Mike Hough and Pat Mayhew. 1985. vi + 115pp. (0 11 341810 2).

86. Implementing crime prevention measures. Tim Hope. 1985. vi + 82pp. (0 11 340812 9).

87. Resettling refugees: the lessons of research. Simon Field. 1985. vi + 66pp. (0 11 340815 3).

88. Investigating burglary: the measurement of police performance. John Burrows. 1986. vi + 36pp. (0 11 340824 2).

89. Personal violence. Roy Walmsley. 1986. vi + 87pp. (0 11 340827 7).

90. Police-public encounters. Peter Southgate. 1986. vi + 150pp. (0 11 340834 X).

91. Grievance procedures in prisons. John Ditchfield and Claire Austin. 1986. vi + 87pp. (0 11 340839 0).

92. The effectiveness of the Forensic Science Service. Malcolm Ramsay. 1987. v + 100pp. (0 11 340842 0).

93. The police complaints procedure: a survey of complainants' views. David Brown. 1987. v + 98pp. (0 11 340853 6).

94. The validity of the reconviction prediction score. Denis Ward. 1987. vi + 46pp. (0 11 340882 X).

95. Economic aspects of the illicit drug market enforcement policies in the United Kingdom. Adam Wagstaff and Alan Maynard. 1988. vii + 156pp. (0 11 340883 8).

96. Schools, disruptive behaviour and deliquency: a review of literature. John Graham. 1988. v + 70pp. (0 11 340887 0).

97. The tape recording of police interviews with suspects: a second interim report. Carole Willis, John Macleod and Peter Naish. 1988. vii + 97pp. (011 340890 0).

98. Triable-either-way cases: Crown Court or magistrate's court. David Riley and Julie Vennard. 1988. v + 52pp. (0 11 340891 9).

99. Directing patrol work: a study of uniformed policing. John Burrows and Helen Lewis. 1988 v + 66pp. (0 11 340891 9).

100. Probation day centres. George Mair. 1988. v + 44pp. (0 11 340894 3).

101. Amusement machines: dependency and delinquency. John Graham. 1988. v + 48pp. (0 11 340895 1).

102. The use and enforcement of compensation orders in magistrates' courts. Tim Newburn. 1988. v + 49pp. (0 11 340 896 X).

103. Sentencing practice in the Crown Court. David Moxon. 1988. v + 90pp. (0 11 340902 8).

104. Detention at the police station under the Police and Criminal Evidence Act 1984. David Brown. 1988. v + 88pp. (0 11340908 7).

105. Changes in rape offences and sentencing. Charles Lloyd and Roy Walmsley. 1989. vi + 53pp. (0 11 340910 9).

106. Concerns about rape. Lorna Smith. 1989. v + 48pp. (0 11 340911 7).

107. Domestic violence. Lorna Smith. 1989. v + 132pp. (0 11 340925 7)

108. Drinking and disorder: a study of non-metropolitan violence. Mary Tuck. 1989. v + 111pp. (011 340926 5).

109. Special security units. Roy Walmsley. 1989. v + 114pp. (0 11 340961 3).

110. Pre-trial delay: the implications of time limits. Patricia Morgan and Julie Vennard. 1989. v + 66pp. (0 11 340964 8).

111. The 1988 British Crime Survey. Pat Mayhew, David Elliott and Lizanne Dowds. 1989. v + 133pp. (0 11 340965 6).

112. The settlement of claims at the Criminal Injuries Compensation Board. Tim Newburn. 1989. v + 40pp. (0 11 340967 2).

113. Race, community groups and service delivery. Hilary Jackson and Simon Field. 1989. v + 62pp. (0 11 340972 9).

114. Money payment supervision orders: probation policy and practice. George Mair and Charles Lloyd. 1989. v + 40pp. (0 11 340971 0).

115. Suicide and self-injury in prison: a literature review. Charles Lloyd. 1990. v + 69pp. (0 11 3409745 5).

116. Keeping in Touch: police-victim communication in two areas. Tim Newburn and Susan Merry. 1990. v + 52pp. (0 11 340974 5).

117. The police and public in England and Wales: a British Crime Survey report. Wesley G. Skogan. 1990. vi + 74pp. (0 11 340995 8).

118. Control in prisons: a review of the literature. John Ditchfield. 1990 (0 11 340996 6).

119. Trends in crime and their interpretation: a study of recorded crime in post-war England and Wales. Simon Field. 1990. (0 11 340994 X).

120. Electronic monitoring: the trials and their results. George Mair and Claire Nee. 1990. v + 79pp. (0 11 340998 2).

121. Drink driving: the effects of enforcement. David Riley. 1991. viii + 78pp. (0 11 340999 0).

122. Managing difficult prisoners: the Parkhurst Special Unit. Roy Walmsley (Ed.) 1991. x + 139pp. (0 11 341008 5).

123. Investigating burglary: the effects of PACE. David Brown. 1991. xii + 106pp. (0 11 341011 5).

124. Traffic policing in changing times. Peter Southgate and Catriona Mirrlees-Black. 1991. viii + 139pp. (0 11 341019 0).

125. Magistrates' court or Crown Court? Mode of trial decisions and sentencing. Carol Hedderman and David Moxon. 1992. vii + 53pp. (0 11 341036 0).

126. Developments in the use of compensation orders in magistrates' courts since October 1988. David Moxon, John Martin Corkery and Carol Hedderman. 1992. x + 48pp. (0 11 341042 5).

127. A comparative study of firefighting arrangements in Britain, Denmark, the Netherlands and Sweden. John Graham, Simon Field, Roger Tarling and Heather Wilkinson. 1992. x + 57pp. (0 11 341043 3).

128. The National Prison Survey 1991: main findings. Roy Walmsley, Liz Howard and Sheila White. 1992. xiv + 82pp. (0 11 341051 4).

129. Changing the Code: police detention under the revised PACE Codes of Practice. David Brown, Tom Ellis and Karen Larcombe. 1992. viii + 122pp. (0 11 341052 2).

130. Car theft: the offender's perspective. Roy Light, Claire Nee and Helen Ingham. 1993. x + 89pp. (0 11 341069 7).

131. Housing, Community and Crime: The Impact of the Priority Estates Project. Janet Foster and Timothy Hope with assistance from Lizanne Dowds and Mike Sutton. 1993. xi + 118. (0 11 341078 6).

132. The 1992 British Crime Survey. Pat Mayhew, Natalie Aye Maung and Catriona Mirrlees-Black. 1993. xiii + 206. (0 11 341094 8).

Research and Planning Unit Papers (RPUP)

1. Uniformed police work and management technology. J. M. Hough. 1980.

2. Supplementary information on sexual offences and sentencing. Roy Walmsley and Karen White. 1980.

3. Board of visitor adjudications. David Smith, Claire Austin and John Ditchfield. 1981.

4. Day centres and probation. Suzan Fairhead, with the assistance of J.Wilkinson-Grey. 1981.

5. Ethnic minorities and complaints against the police. Philip Stevens and Carole Willis. 1982.

6. Crime and public housing. Mike Hough and Pat Mayhew (editors). 1982.

7. Abstracts of race relations research. George Mair and Philip Stevens (editors). 1982.

8. Police probationer training in race relations. Peter Southgate. 1982.

9. The police response to calls from the public. Paul Ekblom and Kevin Heal. 1982.

10. City centre crime: a situational approach to prevention. Malcolm Ramsay. 1982.

11. Burglary in schools: the prospects for prevention. Tim Hope. 1982.

12. Fine enforcement. Paul Softley and David Moxon. 1982.

13. Vietnamese refugees. Peter Jones. 1982.

14. Community resources for victims of crime. Karen Williams. 1983.

15. The use, effectiveness and impact of police stop and search powers. Carole Willis. 1983.

16. Acquittal rates. Sid Butler. 1983.

17. Criminal justice comparisons: the case of Scotland and England and Wales. Lorna J. F. Smith. 1983.

18. Time taken to deal with juveniles under criminal proceedings. Catherine Frankenburg and Roger Tarling. 1983.

19. Civilian review of complaints against the police: a survey of the United States literature. David C. Brown. 1983.

20. Police action on motoring offences. David Riley. 1983.

21. Diverting drunks from the criminal justice system. Sue Kingsley and George Mair. 1983.

22. The staff resource implications of an independent prosecution system. Peter R. Jones. 1983.

23. Reducing the prison population: an exploratory study in Hampshire. David Smith, Bill Sheppard, George Mair, Karen Williams. 1984.

24. Criminal justice system model: magistrates' courts sub-model. Susan Rice. 1984.

25. Measures of police effectiveness and efficiency. Ian Sinclair and Clive Miller. 1984.

26. Punishment practice by prison Boards of Visitors. Susan Iles, Adrienne Connors, Chris May, Joy Mott. 1984.

27. Reparation, conciliation and mediation: current projects and plans in England and Wales. Tony Marshall. 1984.

28. Magistrates' domestic courts: new perspectives. Tony Marshall (editor). 1984.

29. Racism awareness training for the police. Peter Southgate. 1984.

30. Community constables: a study of a policing initiative. David Brown and Susan Iles. 1985.

31. Recruiting volunteers. Hilary Jackson. 1985.

32. Juvenile sentencing: is there a tariff? David Moxon, Peter Jones, Roger Tarling. 1985.

33. Bringing people together: mediation and reparation projects in Great Britain. Tony Marshall and Martin Walpole. 1985.

34. Remands in the absence of the accused. Chris May. 1985.

35. Modelling the criminal justice system. Patricia M. Morgan. 1985.

36. The criminal justice system model: the flow model. Hugh Pullinger. 1986.

37. Burglary: police actions and victim views. John Burrows. 1986.

38. Unlocking community resources: four experimental government small grants schemes. Hilary Jackson. 1986.

39. The cost of discriminating: a review of the literature. Shirley Dex. 1986.

40. Waiting for Crown Court trial: the remand population. Rachel Pearce. 1987.

41. Children's evidence: the need for corroboration. Carol Hedderman. 1987.

42.	A prelimary study of victim offender mediation and reparation schemes in England and Wales. Gwynn Davis, Jacky Boucherat, David Watson, Adrian Thatcher (Consultant). 1987.

43.	Explaining fear of crime: evidence from the 1984 British Crime Survey. Michael Maxfield. 1987.

44.	Judgements of crime seriousness: evidence from the 1984 British Crime Survey. Ken Pease. 1988.

45.	Waiting time on the day in magistrates' courts: a review of case listings practises. David Moxon and Roger Tarling (editors). 1988.

46.	Bail and probation work: the ILPS temporary bail action project. George Mair. 1988.

47.	Police work and manpower allocation. Roger Tarling. 1988.

48.	Computers in the courtroom. Carol Hedderman. 1988.

49.	Data interchange between magistrates' courts and other agencies. Carol Hedderman. 1988.

50.	Bail and probation work II: the use of London probation/bail hostels for bailees. Helen Lewis and George Mair. 1989.

51.	The role and function of police community liaison officers. Susan V. Phillips and Raymond Cochrane. 1989.

52.	Insuring against burglary losses. Helen Lewis. 1989.

53.	Remand decisions in Brighton and Bournemouth. Patricia Morgan and Rachel Pearce. 1989.

54.	Racially motivated incidents reported to the police. Jayne Seagrave. 1989.

55.	Review of research on re-offending of mentally disordered offenders. David J. Murray. 1990.

56.	Risk prediction and probation: papers from a Research and Planning Unit workshop. George Mair (editor). 1990.

57.	Household fires: findings from the British Crime Survey 1988. Chris May. 1990.

58.	Home Office funding of victim support schemes - money well spent? Justin Russell. 1990.

59.	Unit fines: experiments in four courts. David Moxon, Mike Sutton and Carol Hedderman. 1990.

60.	Deductions from benefit for fine default. David Moxon, Carol Hedderman and Mike Sutton. 1990.

PUBLICATIONS

61. Monitoring time limits on custodial remands. Paul F. Henderson. 1991.

62. Remands in custody for up to 28 days: the experiments. Paul F. Henderson and Patricia Morgan. 1991.

63. Parenthood training for young offenders: an evaluation of courses in Young Offender Institutions. Diane Caddle. 1991.

64. The multi-agency approach in practice: the North Plaistow racial harassment project. William Saulsbury and Benjamin Bowling. 1991.

65. Offending while on bail: a survey of recent studies. Patricia M. Morgan. 1992.

66. Juveniles sentenced for serious offences: a comparison of regimes in Young Offender Institutions and Local Authority Community Homes. John Ditchfield and Liza Catan. 1992.

67. The management and deployment of police armed response vehicles. Peter Southgate. 1992.

68. Using psychometric personality tests in the selection of firearms officers. Catriona Mirrlees-Black. 1992.

69. Bail information schemes: practice and effect. Charles Lloyd. 1992.

70. Crack and cocaine in England and Wales. Joy Mott (editor). 1992

71. Rape: from recording to conviction. Sharon Grace, Charles Lloyd and Lorna J.F. Smith. 1992.

72. The National Probation Survey 1990. Chris May. 1993.

73. Public satisfaction with police services. Peter Southgate and Debbie Crisp. 1993.

74. Disqualification from driving: an effective penalty? Catriona Mirrlees-Black. 1993.

75. Detention under the Prevention of Terrorism (Temporary Provisions) Act 1989: Access to legal advice and outside contact. David Brown. 1993.

76. Panel assessment schemes for mentally disordered offenders. Carol Hedderman. 1993.

77. Cash-limiting the probation service: a case study in resource allocation. Simon Field and Mike Hough. 1993.

78. The probation response to drug misuse. Claire Nee and Rae Sibbitt. 1993.

79. Approval of rifle and target shooting clubs: the effects of the new and revised criteria. John Martin Corkery. 1993.

80. The long-term needs of victims: A review of the literature. Tim Newburn. 1993.

81. The welfare needs of unconvicted prisoners. Diane Caddle and Sheila White. 1994.

82. Racially motivated crime: a British Crime Survey analysis. Natalie Aye Maung and Catriona Mirrlees-Black. 1994.

83. Mathematical models for forecasting Passport demand. Andy Jones and John MacLeod. 1994.

84. The theft of firearms. John Corkery. 1994.

85. Equal opportunities and the Fire Service. Tom Bucke. 1994.

86. Not published yet

87. Group 4 Prisoner Escort Service: a survey of customer satisfaction.
Claire Nee. 1994.

Research Findings

(These are summaries of reports and are also available from the Information Section)

1. Magistrates' court or Crown Court? Mode of trial decisions and their impact on sentencing. Carol Hedderman and David Moxon. 1992.

2. Surveying crime: findings from the 1992 British Crime Survey. Pat Mayhew and Natalie Aye Maung. 1992.

3. Car Theft: the offenders's perspective: Claire Nee. 1993.

4. The National Prison survey 1991: main findings. Roy Walmsley, Liz Howard and Sheila White. 1993.

5. Changing the Code: Police detention under the revised PACE codes of practice. David Brown, Tom Ellis and Karen Larcombe. 1993.

6. Rifle and pistol target shooting clubs: The effects of new approval criteria. John M. Corkery. 1993.

7. Self-reported drug misuse in England and Wales. Main findings from the 1992 British Crime Survey. Joy Mott and Catriona Mirrlees-Black. 1993.

8. Findings from the International Crime Survey. Pat Mayhew. 1994.

9. Fear of Crime: Findings from the 1992 British Crime Survey. Catriona Mirrlees-Black and Natalie Aye Maung. 1994.

10. Does the Criminal Justice system treat men and women differently? Carol Hedderman and Mike Hough. 1994.

11. Participation in Neighbourhood Watch: Findings from the 1992 British Crime Survey. Lizanne Dowds and Pat Mayhew. 1994.

12. Not published yet.

13. Equal opportunities and the Fire Service. Tom Bucke. 1994.

14.   Trends in Crime: Findings from the 1994 British Crime Survey. Pat Mayhew, Catriona Mirrlees-Black and Natalie Aye Maung. 1994.

Research Bulletin (available from the Information Section)

The Research Bulletin is published twice a year and consists mainly of short articles relating to projects which are part of the Home Office Research and Planning Unit's research programme.

Occasional Papers

(These can be purchased from the main Home Office Library Publications Unit, 50 Queen Anne's Gate, London SWIH 9AT. Telephone 0171-273 2302 for information on price and availability. Those marked with an asterisk are out of print.)

*The 'watchdog' role of Boards of Visitors. Mike Maguire and Jon Vagg. 1984.

Shared working between Prison and Probation Officers. Norman Jepson and Kenneth Elliot. 1985.

After-care Services for Released Prisoners: A Review of the Literature. Kevin Haines. 1990.

*Arts in Prisons: towards a sense of achievement. Anne Peaker and Jill Vincent. 1990.

Pornography: impacts and influences. Dennis Howitt and Guy Cumberbatch. 1990.

*An evaluation of the live link for child witnesses. Graham Davies and Elizabeth Noon. 1991.

Mentally disordered prisoners. John Gunn, Tony Maden and Mark Swinton. 1991.

Coping with a crisis: the introduction of three and two in a cell. T G Weiler. 1992.

Psychiatric Assessment at the Magistrates' Court. Philip Joseph. 1992.

Measurement of caseload weightings in magistrates' courts. Richard J. Gadsden and Graham J. Worsdale. 1992.

The CDE of scheduling in magistrates' courts. John W. Raine and Michael J. Willson. 1992.

Employment opportunities for offenders. David Downes. 1993.

Sex offenders: a framework for the evaluation of community-based treatment. Mary Barker and Rod Morgan. 1993.

Suicide attempts and self-injury in male prisons. Alison Liebling and Helen Krarup. 1993.

Measurement of caseload weightings associated with the Children's Act. Richard J. Gadsden and Graham J. Worsdale. 1994. (available from the RPU Information Section).

Managing difficult prisoners: The Lincoln and Hull special units.

Professor Keith Bottomley, Professor Norman Jepson, Mr Kenneth Elliott and Dr Jeremy Coid. 1994 (available from RPU Information Section).

The Nacro diversion iniative for mentally disturbed offenders: an account and an evaluation. Home Office, NACRO and Mental Health Foundation (available from Information Section).

Other Publications by members of RPU (available from HMSO)

Designing out crime. R. V. G. Clarke and P. Mayhew (editors). 1980. viii + 186pp. (0 11 340732 7).

Policing today. Kevin Heal, Roger Tarling and John Burrows (editors). v + 181pp. (0 11 340800 5).

Managing criminal justice: a collection of papers. David Moxon (editor). 1985. vi + 222pp. (0 11 340811 0).

Situational crime prevention: from theory into practice. Kevin Heal and Gloria Laycock (editors). 1986. vii + 166pp. (0 11 340826 9).

Communities and crime reduction. Tim Hope and Margaret Shaw (editors). 1988. vii + 311pp. (11 340892 7).

New directions in police training. Peter Southgate (editor). 1988. xi + 256pp (11 340889 7).

Crime and Accountability: Victim/Offender Mediation in Practice. Tony F. Marshall and Susan Merry. 1990. xii + 262. (0 11 340973 7).

Community Work and the Probation Service. Paul Henderson and Sarah del Tufo. 1991. vi + 120. (0 11 341004 2).

Part Time Punishment? George Mair. 1991. 258 pp. (0 11 340981 8).

Analysing Offending. Data, Models and Interpretations. Roger Tarling. 1993. viii + 203. (0 11 341080 8).

Printed in the United Kingdom for HMSO
Dd.0300337, 4/95, C15, 3400, 5673, 319005